TWENTY
LIFE-CHANGING BUDDHIST CONCEPTS

◆

Reprinted From the World Tribune

World Tribune
Press

Published by World Tribune Press
A division of the SGI-USA
606 Wilshire Blvd.
Santa Monica, CA 90401

© 2023 SGI-USA

All rights reserved.
Printed in the United States of America.

Cover artwork by Linda Erwe / EyeEm / Getty Images.
Back cover illustrations by rawpixel.com / Freepik.
interior illustrations by Malte Mueller/ Getty Images.
Cover and interior design by Jocelyn Hsu.

29 28 27 26 25   4 5 6 7 8

ISBN: 978-1-944604-63-9

Library of Congress Control Number: 2023931442

CONTENTS

EDITOR'S NOTE   v

ONE | NAM-MYOHO-RENGE-KYO   1
The Fundamental Power of the Universe

TWO | CHANGING POISON INTO MEDICINE   5
Challenges Can Fortify Our Growth and Happiness

THREE | THE NINE CONSCIOUSNESSES   9
Changing Our Deepest Karma

FOUR | ATTAINING BUDDHAHOOD IN THIS LIFETIME   13
Becoming Buddhas Here and Now

FIVE | BODHISATTVAS OF THE EARTH   17
The Bodhisattva Opens the Way to Happiness for All

SIX | ESTABLISHING THE CORRECT TEACHING FOR THE PEACE OF THE LAND   21
"When We Change, Our Land Will Change"

SEVEN | THE GOHONZON   25
The Mirror That Reflects Our Truest Self

EIGHT | THE FOUR POWERS   29
How to Amplify Our Power of Faith

NINE | THE FUSION OF REALITY AND WISDOM   33
In "Reality," We Are All Buddhas

TEN | CASTING OFF THE TRANSIENT AND REVEALING THE TRUE   37
Breaking Down Barriers, Expanding Our Life State

ELEVEN | CHANGING KARMA   41
Outshining Our Karma With the "Sun of Wisdom"

TWELVE | THE MUTUAL POSSESSION OF THE TEN WORLDS   47
Every Situation Is the Best Situation for Elevating Our Lives

THIRTEEN | THREE THOUSAND REALMS IN A SINGLE MOMENT OF LIFE   51
Tap Your Greatest Potential at Any Moment

FOURTEEN | MANY IN BODY, ONE IN MIND 57
Unity in Diversity

FIFTEEN | FAITH EQUALS DAILY LIFE 61
The Power to Win Each Day

SIXTEEN | ONENESS 65
We Are Connected to Everyone, Everything

SEVENTEEN | ONENESS OF BODY AND MIND 69
Our Resolve Is Everything

EIGHTEEN | ONENESS OF GOOD AND EVIL 73
Transforming Evil Into the Highest Good

NINETEEN | ONENESS OF LIFE AND ITS ENVIRONMENT 77
Winning Over Ourselves Brings Victory in All Other Realms

TWENTY | ONENESS OF MENTOR AND DISCIPLE 81
A Shared Commitment to Elevate Humanity

NOTES 85

EDITOR'S NOTE

Twenty Life-Changing Buddhist Concepts was originally serialized in the *World Tribune* from June 4 to December 10, 2021.

The citations most commonly used in this book have been abbreviated as follows:

LSOC, page number(s) refers to *The Lotus Sutra and Its Opening and Closing Sutras,* translated by Burton Watson (Tokyo: Soka Gakkai, 2009).

OTT, page number(s) refers to *The Record of the Orally Transmitted Teachings,* translated by Burton Watson (Tokyo: Soka Gakkai, 2004).

WND, page number(s) refers to *The Writings of Nichiren Daishonin,* vol. 1 (WND-1) (Tokyo: Soka Gakkai, 1999) and vol. 2 (WND-2) (Tokyo: Soka Gakkai, 2006).

CONCEPT ONE

NAM-MYOHO-RENGE-KYO
The Fundamental Power of the Universe

What is the way to genuine and lasting happiness? Buddhism teaches that we develop true happiness by bringing forth our inherent goodness, or Buddhahood, not only for our own well-being but also for the greater good of humanity.

Nichiren Buddhism offers a way for all of us to reveal our innate Buddhahood and actualize our limitless potential in this lifetime. Regardless of our socioeconomic background, gender, race, education, or experience, we can overcome all suffering and lead the most meaningful, happy, and harmonious lives.

The key to doing all of this starts with chanting Nam-myoho-renge-kyo. President Ikeda explains:

> Our health, courage, wisdom, joy, desire to improve, self-discipline, and so on, could all be said to depend on our life force. Chanting Nam-myoho-renge-kyo enables us to bring forth limitless life force. Those who base themselves on chanting Nam-myoho-renge-kyo are therefore never deadlocked.
> The important thing is to continue chanting every day, no

matter what happens. Nam-myoho-renge-kyo is the fundamental power of the universe.[1]

Let's review some key points about Nam-myoho-renge-kyo, the essence of Nichiren Daishonin's teaching and the fundamental principle for revealing our Buddhahood in this lifetime.

AWAKENING TO THE FUNDAMENTAL LAW PERVADING THE UNIVERSE

Shakyamuni, the founder of Buddhism some twenty-five hundred years ago, recognized that all people endure the four universal sufferings of birth, aging, sickness, and death. He sought a way to relieve these sufferings, and in the process, he awakened to the truth that he possessed within his own life the eternal, fundamental principle, or Law, pervading the universe and all life. He came to be called a Buddha or "awakened one." And to guide many others to the same awakening, he expounded numerous teachings, which were compiled after his death as Buddhist sutras.

Later, in thirteenth-century Japan, Nichiren pored over the many Buddhist scriptures and discovered the essence of the Buddha's teaching in the Lotus Sutra. He identified the Law to which Shakyamuni had awakened as Nam-myoho-renge-kyo. And he taught that this Law is the essential means for attaining Buddhahood and opening the way to lasting happiness.

He writes:

> If you wish to free yourself from the sufferings of birth and death you have endured since time without beginning and to attain without fail unsurpassed enlightenment in this lifetime, you must perceive the mystic truth that is originally inherent in all living beings. This truth is Myoho-renge-kyo. Chanting Myoho-renge-kyo will therefore enable you to grasp the mystic truth innate in all life. (WND-1, 3)

Nichiren established the practice of chanting Nam-myoho-renge-kyo as a concrete means to free ourselves from life's sufferings. By chanting, we bring forth our inherent wisdom to perceive the truth of life and come to understand life from the enlightened perspective of Buddhahood. As a result, we can use everything that comes our way to enhance and strengthen our lives.

THE PROFOUND MEANING OF NAM-MYOHO-RENGE-KYO

A name can convey much about a person, place, or thing. For instance, Nichiren states:

> The two characters that comprise the name Japan contain within them all the people and animals and wealth in the sixty-six provinces of the country, without a single omission. . . .
> The five characters of Myoho-renge-kyo[2] do not represent the sutra text, nor are they its meaning. They are nothing other than the intent of the entire sutra. So, even though beginners in Buddhist practice may not understand their significance, by practicing these five characters, they will naturally conform to the sutra's intent. (WND-1, 788)

The Lotus Sutra's full meaning is reflected in its name, which in Japanese is Myoho-renge-kyo. Loosely translated, this is "Lotus Sutra of the Wonderful Law."

Myo means "mystic" or "wondrous," and *ho* means "law." Together they form *myoho*, often translated as Mystic Law, the fundamental Law of the universe, which is difficult to understand.

Renge means "lotus flower," which symbolizes the wonderful characteristics of the Mystic Law.

The lotus plant grows in muddy swamps yet produces pure and fragrant blooms—just as we practice Buddhism amid our daily challenges and bring forth our pure, inherent goodness: our enlightenment.

Also, the lotus's flowers and fruit develop together, the perfect metaphor for the principle that cause and effect occur simultaneously. President Ikeda says, "Just as the fruit and flowers of the lotus mature at the same time, the effect, or the world of Buddhahood, develops in our lives simultaneously as we carry out our Buddhist practice for the spread of the Law."[3]

Kyo means "sutra" and indicates the teaching that reveals the mystic nature of life, the Lotus Sutra. It also signifies our voice that conveys this teaching.

Finally, *nam* comes from the Sanskrit word *namas*, meaning "bow" or "reverence." It means to "dedicate one's life" and points to having faith in the Mystic Law.

Nichiren writes:

> The Lotus Sutra is the king of sutras, the direct path to enlightenment, for it explains that the entity of our life, which manifests either good or evil at each moment, is in fact the entity of the Mystic Law.
>
> If you chant Myoho-renge-kyo with deep faith in this principle, you are certain to attain Buddhahood in this lifetime. (WND-1, 4)

Nichiren awakened to the truth that his own life was itself the Mystic Law as were the lives of all others. He revealed this truth in the teaching and practice of chanting Nam-myoho-renge-kyo, a simple practice anyone can do.

By chanting Nam-myoho-renge-kyo and sharing it with others, we carry on his legacy, which is to establish the path for us all to transform our lives and our world, and create a bright future for humanity. This is the way to genuine and lasting happiness for everyone.

CONCEPT TWO

CHANGING POISON INTO MEDICINE
Challenges Can Fortify Our Growth and Happiness

"**My daughter and I** weren't very close, and she wasn't excited to come home from college to quarantine with her parents," says an SGI-USA men's division member. "Seeking a way to connect with her, I chanted Nam-myoho-renge-kyo to change this poison into medicine. We started taking evening walks together, discussing our favorite movies and albums. Yesterday, I overheard her tell a classmate, 'My dad is my new best friend.'"

His determination to "change poison into medicine" exemplifies the resolve of other SGI members, who, like many struggling amid the longstanding global pandemic, grapple with losing loved ones, face financial struggles, and take on various challenges. They have repeatedly proven that our worst suffering can be the greatest catalyst for creating lasting happiness.

A character in *The Count of Monte Cristo*, Abbé Faria, expresses this ideal: "Misfortune is needed to plumb certain mysterious depths in the understanding of men; pressure is needed to explode the charge.... The clash of clouds produces electricity, electricity produces lightning and lightning gives light."[1]

CHANGING THE THREE PATHS INTO THE THREE VIRTUES

The character *myo* in the Lotus Sutra's title can mean "wonderful" or "mystic." The great Buddhist scholar Nagarjuna[2] explains that this character *myo* is "like a great physician who can change poison into medicine" (WND-2, 743).

Regarding this, Nichiren Daishonin writes:

> What is the poison? It is the three paths of earthly desires, karma, and suffering that are our lot. What is the medicine? It is the Dharma body, wisdom, and emancipation. And what does it mean to change poison into medicine? It means to transform the three paths into the three virtues. (WND-2, 743)

Here, poison refers to the "three paths": "earthly desires," fueled by deluded impulses of greed, anger, and foolishness; "karma," negative actions driven by desires; and "suffering" arising from earthly desires and karma. This negative cycle gives rise to lives shackled in misery, despite people's best efforts to improve.

While other schools of Buddhism teach that we must eliminate desires, karma, and suffering to attain enlightenment, Nichiren teaches that, by chanting Nam-myoho-renge-kyo, we transform the poison of our desires into the medicine of the three virtues. These virtues are the "Dharma body," the Law, or truth, to which Buddhas are awakened; "wisdom," the capacity to manifest and use the Law in our lives; and "emancipation," the state of inner freedom unswayed by the sufferings of birth and death.

President Ikeda says:

> The Mystic Law enables ordinary people whose lives are filled with delusion to attain Buddhahood just as they are, without eradicating desire and suffering. . . .
>
> Though we may find ourselves suffering, confused, or troubled because of earthly desires, when we illuminate our lives with

the wisdom of enlightenment, we can move in the direction of hope and change poison into medicine.

By recognizing our earthly desires and sufferings for what they are and facing them head-on, we can reveal our innate Buddhahood and establish a state of happiness.[3]

Hardships are inevitable. But by activating our inherent Buddha nature, we can resolve any and all obstacles. Rather than resenting difficulties, we view them as opportunities to tap our inner reserves of hope, courage, compassion, creativity, and all of our enlightened attributes.

CONCEPT THREE

THE NINE CONSCIOUSNESSES
Changing Our Deepest Karma

What distinguishes Nichiren Buddhism from other religions and philosophies? We could say it is the view that every person, without exception, possesses the Buddha nature, or the potential to be a fully awakened human being.

Both the causes and solutions to our problems are found within us. Often what causes us to suffer is negative karma, the latent effects of negative causes we've made in past lifetimes until today. Karma can be likened to a raging river's currents that are hard to resist, even when solutions to our problems seem clear.

Chanting Nam-myoho-renge-kyo is the most powerful means for bringing forth the overriding power of our Buddha nature and transforming our negative karma.

While the Buddha nature is described in many ways in various Buddhist sutras and teachings, one view associates it with the ninth or deepest level of consciousness.

President Ikeda explains: "The ninth consciousness is itself the ultimate reality of all things and is equivalent to the universal Buddha nature. Buddhism teaches that we can change our deepest karma through drawing upon this inner capacity of our lives."[1]

Let's briefly study the nine levels of consciousness.

THE DYNAMICS OF CHANGING KARMA

The principle of the nine consciousnesses teaches that we can change any and all karma.

The first five of the nine consciousnesses are related directly to our five senses: sight, hearing, smell, taste, and touch. The sixth, called mind-consciousness, integrates the information from the five senses and processes how we perceive our surroundings.

These first six levels, our conscious realm, represent the awareness with which we process the outside world, an awareness influenced and sometimes distorted by what is going on in our deeper levels of consciousness.

The next three levels deal with these deeper levels. The seventh, called *mano*-consciousness, is said to be where self-awareness or ego originates and where our subconscious impulses, including the impulse for self-preservation, are found.

The eighth level is called *alaya*-consciousness. The Sanskrit word *alaya* means "repository" or "storehouse," thus it is also called the karmic storehouse. It is where the effects of all our thoughts, words, and deeds from past lifetimes to the present reside in latent, or potential, form until they appear.

As an example, if we mistrust people due to past experiences, we may try to shield ourselves from being hurt (*mano*-consciousness). This may lead to perceiving others as untrustworthy or hesitating to share our honest thoughts (first six levels of consciousness). Our thoughts, words, and actions in this regard remain imprinted in our lives (*alaya*-consciousness). These in turn may influence our awareness, actions, and the future, leading to a cycle of suffering.

This is where the ninth consciousness, called the *amala*-consciousness, comes into play. The Sanskrit word *amala* means "pure," and it indicates a level of consciousness that is unsullied by karmic impurities.

Chanting Nam-myoho-renge-kyo can be likened to drilling through the layers of karma and delusion found in the other levels of consciousness and striking the pure wisdom of the ninth consciousness, which can wash away all impurities.

Nichiren advises, "You should base your mind on the ninth consciousness, and carry out your practice in the six consciousnesses" (WND-1, 458). Regarding this passage, President Ikeda says:

> By establishing faith in the ultimate reality and incorporating Buddhist practice into our daily lives, we can access infinite wisdom, power, and compassion; we can achieve a fundamental inner reformation and establish an unshakable foundation for true happiness. By analogy, while a piece of wood floating in a stream will be swept away at the whim of the current, even the most powerful of currents cannot shift an island of rock.[2]

TRANSFORMING THE KARMA OF HUMANITY

While the first seven consciousnesses are said to disappear when we die, the eighth and ninth persist. They define our lives as we traverse the cycle of birth and death. This might explain why we can see certain patterns throughout history that extend beyond individuals and expand to all humankind.

For instance, despite significant advances in science, economics, and many other fields, the impulse of greed has worsened the global environmental crisis we now face and the great disparities in wealth. President Ikeda explains:

> Our karmic energy mutually impacts our loved ones (living and deceased) and indeed all humankind. It even affects animals and plants. A positive change in the karmic energy in the depths of one's life becomes the cogwheel for change in the lives of others.[3]

When based on the ninth consciousness, we can view all our karmic impediments as cogwheels for manifesting our Buddhahood. By chanting, we not only gain complete control of our lives but also bring forth the wisdom, courage, and compassion to create a world based on the Buddhist ideals of respect, equality, and the interconnectedness of life.

ATTAINING BUDDHAHOOD IN THIS LIFETIME
Becoming Buddhas Here and Now

Most of us probably began practicing Buddhism to overcome some problem or achieve a dream that seemed out of reach. Becoming enlightened, or "attaining Buddhahood," may not have been high up on our list.

No matter why we started, however, attaining Buddhahood—a deep, indestructible kind of happiness—remains the primary goal of Nichiren Buddhist practice. And herein lies Nichiren Buddhism's revolutionary view of Buddhahood: each person, no matter who, has a Buddha nature.

Nichiren Buddhism also teaches the principle of attaining Buddhahood in this lifetime. Other Buddhist schools teach that becoming a Buddha is something far removed from daily life, something that happens only after we die or after an interminable period of intense Buddhist practices over countless lifetimes.

Fortunately, Nichiren Buddhism gives us the means to become a Buddha in this life.

"NOT A ONE WILL FAIL TO ATTAIN BUDDHAHOOD"

Nichiren Daishonin talks about a passage from "Expedient Means," the second chapter of the Lotus Sutra: "If there are those who hear the Law, then not a one will fail to attain Buddhahood" (LSOC, 75).

"This passage," he says, "means that, if there are a hundred or a thousand people who uphold this sutra, without a single exception all one hundred or one thousand of them will become Buddhas" (WND-1, 1099).

The title "Buddha" means "awakened one" and refers to the state of life—rich with wisdom, compassion, courage, and confidence—of a fully awakened individual.

Nichiren taught that anyone can fully access this awakened state. In fact, we can tap it right this instant by chanting Nam-myoho-renge-kyo to the Gohonzon.

So if all people naturally possess the world of Buddhahood what, then, does it mean to "attain Buddhahood"?

"'Attain' means to open or reveal" (OTT, 126), Nichiren says.

We can open the Buddha nature that is within us right here and now, just as we are. That is, even if we're in a state of suffering, by chanting Nam-myoho-renge-kyo, we can bring forth hope and confidence.

Thus, enlightenment isn't something we gain or receive in the distant future, nor is a Buddha a special, superhuman being. Attaining Buddhahood means awakening the wondrous inner qualities we naturally possess. It also means to live in the most fulfilling way, a way unique and true to ourselves.

HUMAN REVOLUTION: A MODERN EXPRESSION OF BUDDHAHOOD

Revealing our Buddhahood through chanting is also a process of purifying our lives, fully displaying and putting to best use our inherent power. Through this process, we bring forth our strongest life force, leaving us unhindered by any hardship or opposition. In fact, by chanting about and taking action to resolve our challenges, we further purify and strengthen our lives, gaining greater physical and mental well-being.

Second Soka Gakkai president Josei Toda described attaining Buddhahood as "human revolution," an ongoing process of profound personal growth.

President Ikeda has suggested seven indicators by which we can measure our human revolution: health, youthfulness, good fortune, wisdom, passion, conviction, and victory.

He highlighted "the development of compassion as an essential foundation . . . that encompasses all seven elements."[1]

"Life Span," the Lotus Sutra's sixteenth chapter, ends with Shakyamuni Buddha's statement "At all times I think to myself: How can I cause living beings to gain entry into the unsurpassed way and quickly acquire the body of a Buddha?" (LSOC, 273). Here, "body" can mean "identity" or "self."

So he wishes to enable each person to become a Buddha. This expresses not only the Buddha's compassion but his strong sense of responsibility to help everyone become happy.

The Soka Gakkai today is the gathering of people dedicated to realizing this wish and vow of Shakyamuni and Nichiren. On a broader scale, we call this kosen-rufu.

President Ikeda writes:

> When we take on problems and challenges, chant Nam-myoho-renge-kyo, and make efforts based on a great sense of responsibility for kosen-rufu, the life state of Buddhahood, of Nam-myoho-renge-kyo, that the Daishonin embodied cannot fail to manifest itself in our lives.[2]

Maybe attaining Buddhahood wasn't tops on our list when we started chanting. But as we advance in our Buddhist practice, we can develop our abilities to truly care about others, about kosen-rufu and peace, and savor genuine, enduring happiness.

BODHISATTVAS OF THE EARTH
The Bodhisattva Opens the Way to Happiness for All

Why was I born? What is the purpose of my life? People throughout history, from philosophers to everyday folks, have grappled with such existential questions.

Buddhism's answer is that we're here to become absolutely happy as we overcome every kind of challenge, develop resilient, joyful lives, and open the way to happiness for others as well. This is what Buddhism calls the bodhisattva way.

President Ikeda explains:

> We must open our eyes to the infinite potential that every person possesses. Religion's mission, in the broadest sense, is to conquer the ego and motivate us to serve and encourage one another.
>
> The social practice of the bodhisattva way of Mahayana Buddhism, based on the philosophy of the sanctity of life, is to boldly, courageously strive in our daily lives to overcome self-interest, contribute to others and to society, live a good life, and elevate ourselves.[1]

In the Lotus Sutra, the Bodhisattvas of the Earth are ideal examples of the way. They appear in "Emerging from the Earth," the sutra's fifteenth chapter. Other disciples have volunteered to fulfill the mission to propagate the Mystic Law after the Buddha's passing. In a dramatic turn, however, Shakyamuni Buddha discloses that he has long been training a yet-unknown group of bodhisattvas "who are as numerous as the sands of sixty thousand Ganges Rivers" and who "will be able to protect, embrace, read, recite, and widely spread this sutra" (LSOC, 252).

At that moment, the ground trembles and splits open, and millions of resplendent bodhisattvas dance forth from the opening, ready to carry out their mission to propagate the Lotus Sutra in the most troubled times after the Buddha's passing (today).

President Ikeda says: "It seems that 'dancing forth' is a fitting image for the appearance of the Bodhisattvas of the Earth. . . . They don't come forth reluctantly because Shakyamuni told them to; rather [they] leap forth and dance exuberantly with the sense: 'Our time has come at last!'"[2]

WHAT ARE THE ATTRIBUTES OF THE BODHISATTVAS OF THE EARTH?

Nichiren Daishonin was convinced that his personal mission accorded with that of a Bodhisattva of the Earth; he devoted himself to his bodhisattva vow to joyfully spread the Lotus Sutra and lead all people to enlightenment.

He faced intense, life-threatening ordeals to establish his teaching of Nam-myoho-renge-kyo, which, almost eight hundred years later, continues to empower people around the globe, a testament to its enduring universality.

So how does this ideal of the Bodhisattvas of the Earth relate to our own lives? In the same spirit as these bodhisattvas and Nichiren, we practice Buddhism to live the most fulfilling and beneficial lives for ourselves and others. Let's take a look at a handful of the many splendid qualities of these bodhisattvas that Nichiren discusses and that we can bring forth in our lives.

1. *"The function of fire is to burn and give light"* (WND-1, 218). As courageous bodhisattvas, we use our suffering as fuel to "burn," transforming it into the light of wisdom to show others how to move forward in life, undefeated by anything.

2. *"The function of water is to wash away filth"* (WND-1, 218). We purify our lives by chanting Nam-myoho-renge-kyo. Remaining unsullied by the delusions and challenges of everyday life and society, we face things head-on, spreading our pure, vibrant attitude to all around us.

3. *"The winds blow away dust and breathe life into plants, animals, and human beings"* (WND-1, 218). Nichiren Buddhists are never defeated by obstacles. We infuse people with fresh energy by clearing away all negative functions as if they were no more "than dust before the wind" (WND-1, 280).

4. *"The earth produces the grasses and trees, and heaven provides nourishing moisture"* (WND-1, 218). Like the earth that supports all plants and the rains that nourish them, we believe that all people are equally endowed with the Buddha nature, and we embrace everyone with warm encouragement while working to build a society of peace, respect, and harmonious coexistence in which everyone can prosper.

President Ikeda says:

> We have chosen, in accord with our vow as bodhisattvas, to be born into the evil age of the Latter Day of the Law with all sorts of destinies, or karma—illness, financial hardship, family discord, loneliness, low self-esteem, and the list goes on—to help guide others to enlightenment. But by chanting Nam-myoho-renge-kyo, striving in our Buddhist practice for ourselves and others, and dedicating our lives to kosen-rufu, our vibrant life force as Bodhisattvas of the Earth and the expansive life state of

Bodhisattvas of the Earth **19**

Buddhahood well forth within us. Our lives will brim with the wisdom, courage, strength, hope, and joy to overcome every hardship and daunting obstacle that arises. As we bravely triumph over the onslaughts of karma, we demonstrate the validity of the teachings of Nichiren Buddhism and the tremendous benefit of our Buddhist practice, and we further advance kosen-rufu.[3]

When we awaken to our identity as Bodhisattvas of the Earth, we will find the answers to our questions of why we are here and thus provide hope for others.

CONCEPT SIX

ESTABLISHING THE CORRECT TEACHING FOR THE PEACE OF THE LAND
"When We Change, Our Land Will Change"

On July 16, 1260, Nichiren Daishonin submitted his hallmark treatise "On Establishing the Correct Teaching for the Peace of the Land" to Hojo Tokiyori, Japan's de facto ruler. This work takes the form of a dialogue between a host and guest, representing Nichiren and Tokiyori, respectively. At the end of their dialogue, they resolve to work together for the people's happiness.

Q: Why should I care about a treatise written more than 750 years ago?
A: In the opening lines, Nichiren Daishonin describes the conditions in thirteenth-century Japan:

> In recent years, there have been unusual disturbances in the heavens, strange occurrences on earth, famine and pestilence, all affecting every corner of the empire and spreading throughout the land. . . . Over half the population has already been carried off by death, and there is hardly a single person who does not grieve. (WND-1, 6)

Over seven centuries later, we continue to face similar challenges. The principles taught in this treatise can guide us as we address our society's problems and work for peace and happiness.

Q: What does it mean "to establish the correct teaching"?

A: "To establish the correct teaching" first means to apply in our own lives the Lotus Sutra's teaching that all people possess the Buddha nature. And by developing the conviction in this teaching and sharing it with others, we can make this belief society's foundation.

But this is easier said than done. It requires committed effort. That's why Nichiren urges, "Quickly reform the tenets that you hold in your heart and embrace the one true vehicle, the single good doctrine [of the Lotus Sutra]" (WND-1, 25).

For us today, embracing the Lotus Sutra means chanting Nam-myoho-renge-kyo, the sutra's essence, and upholding the belief that all people are worthy of utmost respect. The practice of chanting and sharing Buddhism helps us break through our preconceived ideas and prejudices and develop expansive hearts concerned for the happiness of all humanity.

Of course, not everyone has to chant. Rather, we aim to make the Lotus Sutra's life-affirming philosophy the underpinning of society. As founding Soka Gakkai president Tsunesaburo Makiguchi says, we are engaging in the "process of purifying the negative ideas and thinking that prevail in the Latter Day of the Law . . . with the truth of Nam-myoho-renge-kyo."[1]

Q: What are some actions I can take toward this ideal?

A: When we change, our land will change. No matter how much science, technology, or laws develop, without a fundamental shift in our hearts, we cannot transform our society. Improving ourselves and contributing to others' happiness are key to this shift. Here are three ways we can foster positive change:

1. *Chant Nam-myoho-renge-kyo for a peaceful society.* Our own happiness is inseparable from the happiness of others. President Ikeda says:

The key to establishing peace and prosperity in our world . . . lies in the human heart. . . . . A person who prays for a peaceful and secure society and is considerate toward others will naturally become aware of the need to contribute to society and will act on that awareness.[2]

2. *Share Buddhism.* Sharing Buddhism with others is a courageous act that enables us to deepen our concern for those around us and create trusting relationships. President Ikeda says:

> The important thing, first and foremost, is to chant seriously to share Nam-myoho-renge-kyo with those who are struggling or suffering. Then go out and speak about Nichiren Buddhism with people around you with sincerity and confidence.[3]

3. *Foster capable individuals.* At the end of the treatise, the guest awakens to a vow "to bring peace to the world without delay" by sharing what he has learned from the host (see WND-1, 26).

One committed person can inspire countless others. President Ikeda says:

> If one nurtures a single seed, it will grow into a plant and in turn produce many seeds; each of those seeds is the source for a generation of countless more. In the same way, everything begins with one individual.[4]

Through our daily efforts in faith, in challenging to improve ourselves and in helping others, we can create a bright future of harmony, understanding, respect, and hope for all humankind.

CONCEPT SEVEN

THE GOHONZON
The Mirror That Reflects Our Truest Self

Words on paper can carry great weight and value: A love letter can make our hearts soar. A will of a deceased wealthy uncle can bring about serious family drama. Finding a $100 bill on the sidewalk can make us feel super lucky.

The Gohonzon, the object of devotion in our Buddhist practice, consists of words on paper.

Briefly explaining the Gohonzon, President Ikeda says: "A map is just paper. But if we trust in the map and use it, we will arrive at our intended destination. The Gohonzon is the object of devotion for bringing forth a great state of life so that we can become genuinely happy."[1]

Nichiren Daishonin inscribed the Gohonzon as a visual representation of the Mystic Law, the fundamental Law or truth of all life and the universe. Chanting Nam-myoho-renge-kyo to the Gohonzon enables each of us to dynamically fuse our individual existence with the great life force of the entire universe and develop a life of unshakable happiness.

Let's go over some basics about the Gohonzon.

WHAT IS THE GOHONZON?

The Gohonzon concretely expresses Nichiren's awakening to the Mystic Law of Nam-myoho-renge-kyo. He was the first to teach the chanting of Nam-myoho-renge-kyo, which literally means devotion to Myoho-renge-kyo (Lotus Sutra of the Wonderful Law)—the title of the Lotus Sutra, Shakyamuni Buddha's highest teaching. A sutra's title contains its essence, Nichiren believed, and he added *nam* to signify dedication to this sutra, which teaches that all people equally possess the Buddha nature.

He declares: "I, Nichiren, have inscribed my life in sumi ink, so believe in the Gohonzon with your whole heart. The Buddha's will is the Lotus Sutra, but the soul of Nichiren is nothing other than Nam-myoho-renge-kyo" (WND-1, 412).

On the Gohonzon, Nichiren uses Chinese and Sanskrit characters to depict the Lotus Sutra's Ceremony in the Air.[2] Down the center are the Chinese characters for Nam-myoho-renge-kyo, representing the treasure tower, the ceremony's centerpiece, which symbolizes the world of Buddhahood.

"In the Latter Day of the Law," Nichiren says, "no treasure tower exists other than the figures of the men and women who embrace the Lotus Sutra" (WND-1, 299).

The Gohonzon expresses the reality that all people, without exception, can reveal their inherent Buddhahood by chanting Nam-myoho-renge-kyo.

WHAT IS THE SIGNIFICANCE OF THE GOHONZON?

While we use mirrors to reflect our physical appearance, what can we use to see the inner workings of our heart and mind?

The Gohonzon serves as a mirror that reflects our internal life condition. As the crystallization of the Buddha's wisdom, it helps us clearly see and bring forth the ultimate truth that the Buddha's virtues of compassion, wisdom, and courage exist in our lives.

"Never seek this Gohonzon outside yourself," Nichiren writes.

"The Gohonzon exists only within the mortal flesh of us ordinary people who embrace the Lotus Sutra and chant Nam-myoho-renge-kyo" (WND-1, 832).

By chanting to the Gohonzon, we can tap our truest self and bring forth the immense power from within, while putting our lives in sync with the rhythm of the universe, with our surroundings.

In the mirror of the Gohonzon, "the Buddha," rather than being a distant deity or ideal, is the noblest state of life we can all strive to actualize amid our daily realities.

HOW DO WE USE THE GOHONZON?

To experience the most effective results in chanting to the Gohonzon, we must be aware of what's in our hearts when we pray and strive to orient our prayers toward becoming happy and helping others do the same.

If we pray to the Gohonzon as if begging for aid or if we chant reluctantly, filled with doubt and complaint, President Ikeda explains, "that state of mind is precisely reflected on the entire universe, as if on the surface of a clear mirror."[3]

He continues:

> On the other hand, when you stand up with strong confidence, you will accrue limitless blessings. While controlling your mind, which is at once both extremely subtle and solemnly profound, you should strive to elevate your faith with freshness and vigor. When you do so, both your life and your surroundings will open wide before you, and every action you take will become a source of benefit.[4]

Chanting each day to the Gohonzon is a process of overcoming negativity and bringing forth the most positive determination to break through any deadlock. The more we repeat this process, the more easily it will become to act based on this determination and positively transform each situation with the wisdom, compassion, courage, and life force that emanate from our inherent Buddhahood.

Nichiren inscribed the Gohonzon with the resolve to lead all people to happiness. He also described it as "the banner of propagation of the Lotus Sutra" (WND-1, 831). In other words, the Gohonzon is a tool that helps us propagate the Lotus Sutra's teachings and demonstrate our limitless potential to create happy, fulfilling lives.

Despite tremendous opposition to his propagation efforts, Nichiren never wavered. As President Ikeda writes:

> In teaching the Law and overcoming persecution, Nichiren Daishonin himself manifested the life of the Buddha of limitless joy—the Buddha who has been enlightened since time without beginning and is one with the eternal Law. That is, we can attain the life condition of the Buddha of limitless joy enlightened since time without beginning through our actions, words, and thoughts. This is the state of life inscribed in the Gohonzon.[5]

Following the "map to happiness" that is the Gohonzon surely will be life changing. As we align our prayers with Nichiren's vow for kosen-rufu crystallized in the Gohonzon, chanting ourselves, and sharing this practice with others, we, too, can transform all our negativity and suffering into the fuel for leading lives of limitless joy.

CONCEPT EIGHT

THE FOUR POWERS
How to Amplify Our Power of Faith

From time immemorial, people have prayed, appealing to nature and forces thought greater than themselves for safety, sustenance, happiness, and more. Religion is said to have emerged from this innate impulse to pray.

As Nichiren Buddhists, we don't pray for salvation from external forces. Rather, we pray to fuse the microcosm of our individual lives with the greater macrocosm of the universe. By chanting Nam-myoho-renge-kyo, the fundamental Law that governs all life, we harmonize our lives with the universe.

While it's natural to seek practical, external solutions to our problems, Nichiren Buddhism teaches that by tapping the "four powers of the Mystic Law," we can bring about the best results in any situation, reaffirm the limitless power of our own lives, and enjoy absolute fulfillment and happiness.

WHAT ARE THE FOUR POWERS?

The four powers, essential to realizing our prayers, are:

- **The power of the Buddha:** the Buddha's compassion and wish for the happiness of all people. This is also the abundant wisdom, courage, compassion, and more that exist within us.

- **The power of the Law:** the Mystic Law—the fundamental Law of the universe that is inherent in our lives and permeates all our surroundings—with its immeasurable capacity to lead all people to enlightenment.

- **The power of faith:** our conviction in the Gohonzon, the object of devotion that represents the power of the Buddha and the power of the Law.

- **The power of practice:** chanting Nam-myoho-renge-kyo for ourselves and others, taking action to share this Buddhism, and working for the progress and prosperity of all those around us.

Putting the powers of faith and practice into full gear activates the powers of the Buddha and the Law, resulting in astounding results and benefits. As with anything in life, we get out of our Buddhist practice what we put into it.

President Ikeda explains:

> Just as there are physical laws such as those governing electricity . . . Buddhism delves into and uncovers the Law of life and the universe. Just as the electric light was invented based on the laws of electricity, Nichiren inscribed the Gohonzon based on the supreme Law that Buddhism reveals.
>
> [Second Soka Gakkai president Josei Toda] used to describe the Gohonzon this way: "This certainly doesn't do it full justice, but the Gohonzon can be likened to a happiness-manufacturing machine." The Gohonzon is the ultimate crystallization of human wisdom and the Buddha wisdom. That's why the power of the Buddha and the Law emerge in exact accord with the power of your faith and practice. If the power of your faith and

practice equal a force of one hundred, then they will bring forth the power of the Buddha and the Law to the degree of one hundred. And if it is a force of ten thousand, then it will elicit that degree of corresponding power.[1]

KEEP CHANTING, NO MATTER WHAT

Developing faith doesn't happen overnight—we deepen it by challenging and transforming our tendencies to give in to defeat, anxiety, or fear, and by working to realize our goals and dreams. As we overcome each hurdle, we improve our ability to use our faith and practice to better navigate life's ups and downs.

President Ikeda writes:

> The important thing is to continue chanting daimoku [Nam-myoho-renge-kyo], no matter what. Whether our prayers are answered right away or not, we must keep chanting Nam-myoho-renge-kyo, without harboring any doubts. Those who maintain such faith will eventually attain the supreme path and highest pinnacle of value and savor the conviction that everything unfolded in the very best and most meaningful way. . . . Such are the workings of the Mystic Law and the power of faith.[2]

Facing problems is natural. So is having doubts and uncertainties. The key is to not "harbor" or hold on to such things. By developing our powers of faith and practice, we will replace doubt with confidence, negativity with optimism.

As we study Nichiren Buddhism, we learn how to live based on the hope-filled perspective of Buddhism. And as we chant and take action for the happiness of those around us, we discover the joy of supporting others, deepening our conviction in our own humanity and power.

The life-changing concept of the four powers teaches that it's all up to us. The greater the conviction with which we pray and act, the more strongly the Mystic Law and our surroundings respond.

By aligning our heartfelt prayers with resolute actions, we can break through any deadlock and attain a state of life of complete freedom and happiness.

CONCEPT NINE

THE FUSION OF REALITY AND WISDOM
In "Reality," We Are All Buddhas

We sometimes aren't aware that everyone doesn't view things exactly as we do. Two people can look at the same thing or event and see something entirely different. We may be aghast at a person's failure to see the obvious, but the feeling may be mutual.

Though we like to think of reality, truth, and facts as indisputable, they're often open to interpretation. People filter everything they see, hear, touch, taste, smell, and think through their unique perceptive lenses. Experiences, ingrained beliefs, and from the Buddhist view, their karma—the sum of one's actions over countless lifetimes until now—form these lenses.

Buddhism prescribes the lens of wisdom as the most accurate and valuable way to view reality. Wisdom in this context can be described as the capacity to assess reality unobstructed by prejudices or self-interests. In Nichiren Buddhism, the ultimate relationship between wisdom and reality is "the fusion of reality and wisdom."

Nichiren Daishonin explains:

> Reality means the true nature of all phenomena, and wisdom

means the illuminating and manifesting of this true nature. Thus when the riverbed of reality is infinitely broad and deep, the water of wisdom will flow ceaselessly. When this reality and wisdom are fused, one attains Buddhahood in one's present form. (WND-1, 746)

In general, "wisdom" refers to the cognitive capacity of the mind, and "reality," the object of that cognition, that is, whatever we focus our attention on.

BECOME INDISPENSABLE WHERE YOU ARE

Second Soka Gakkai president Josei Toda explained that we can apply this concept to our daily lives:

> If being a grocer is your "reality," then working hard to make your business prosper is manifesting the "fusion of reality and wisdom."[1]

President Ikeda further explains that our role in life is our "reality":

> It is the light of wisdom that causes this reality to shine. Effecting the perfect fusion of reality and wisdom in our lives means becoming indispensable wherever we are.[2]

The broader our wisdom, the more profoundly we can grasp the import of our reality.

A Buddha is someone who possesses the highest form of wisdom—the wisdom to comprehend the profound, sublime, and eternal Law that pervades the entire universe, the Mystic Law.

Because the Mystic Law is vast, deep, and eternal, the wisdom to fathom it must accordingly be immense and profound.

With such wisdom, we can freely grasp and make best use of the Mystic Law to create an indestructible state of happiness for ourselves and for others.

THE GOHONZON: AN EXPRESSION OF THE FUSION OF REALITY AND WISDOM

Nichiren Daishonin awakened to the wisdom to perceive the eternal life state of Buddhahood, which he taught was the Mystic Law, Nam-myoho-renge-kyo.

He inscribed this state of life in the form of the Gohonzon to which Nichiren Buddhists chant. The Gohonzon graphically embodies the fusion of reality and wisdom.

We may not consider ourselves exceptionally wise, and Buddhism teaches that, these days, no one is truly wise by nature. Fortunately, it also teaches that we ordinary people can "substitute faith for wisdom" (WND-1, 785). That is, when we make the Gohonzon our "reality" and chant Nam-myoho-renge-kyo to it with faith, the life state of the Buddha embodying the fusion of reality and wisdom emerges in our lives.

President Ikeda explains:

> In essence, everyone is a Buddha. That is our "reality." It is the light of wisdom that causes the world of Buddhahood in our lives to shine. Our Buddhahood starts shining when we develop the wisdom to realize we are Buddhas. This is the fusion of reality and wisdom. From our standpoint, according to the Buddhist principle of "substituting faith for wisdom," wisdom means faith. That we possess the world of Buddhahood is the objective truth, the reality, of our lives. Faith causes this reality to shine in actuality.[3]

In a nutshell, the surest way to fuse reality and wisdom is to take the time to chant Nam-myoho-renge-kyo to the Gohonzon. As we chant each day about our troubles and aspirations, we can tap our Buddhahood and find the wisdom for using everything we face to elevate and enrich our lives.

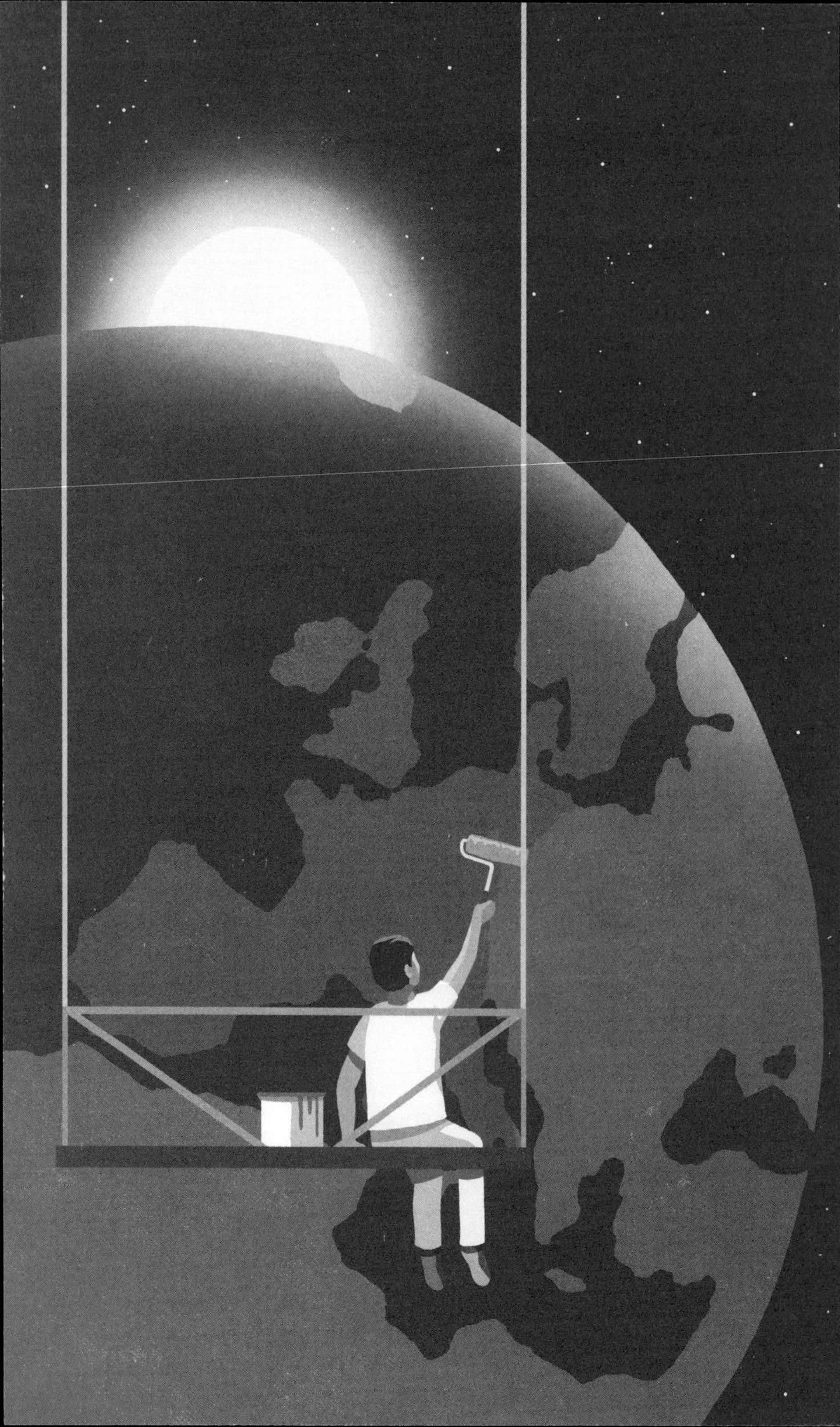

CONCEPT TEN

CASTING OFF THE TRANSIENT AND REVEALING THE TRUE
Breaking Down Barriers, Expanding Our Life State

Nichiren Daishonin faced one of the greatest trials of his life on September 12, 1271. Known as the Tatsunokuchi Persecution, it took place following nearly two decades of tremendous opposition to his efforts to spread the life-affirming teachings of the Lotus Sutra.

After spurious allegations were lodged against Nichiren, he was called in for questioning by Hei no Saemon, the defacto ruler of the Kamakura military government. Nichiren infuriated Hei no Saemon with his warnings that Japan would face ruin if it continued rejecting the correct teaching.

Two days later, on September 12, Hei no Saemon led several hundred soldiers to arrest Nichiren. At midnight, they took him to the beach at Tatsunokuchi to be beheaded.

Nichiren later wrote:

> Finally we came to a place that I knew must be the site of my execution. Indeed, the soldiers stopped and began to mill around in excitement. Saemon-no-jo,[1] in tears, said, "These are your last moments!" I replied, "You don't understand! What greater joy could there be?" (WND-1, 767)

"What greater joy could there be?"—these words illustrate Nichiren's towering state of life. This joy came from giving his life for the Lotus Sutra, which he knew would enable him to reveal his Buddhahood. "If I am to lose this worthless head [for Buddhahood]," he writes, "it will be like trading sand for gold or rocks for jewels" (WND-1, 766).

On the execution grounds, just before the soldier raised his sword, a bright object flew across the sky, terrifying the soldiers to the point that they refused to carry out the execution. A month later, Nichiren was exiled to Sado Island.

Later, recounting the events at Tatsunokuchi, Nichiren says: "On the twelfth day of the ninth month of last year . . . this person named Nichiren was beheaded. It is his soul that has come to this island of Sado" (WND-1, 269).

This statement suggests that Nichiren the ordinary person—through joyfully upholding his belief while facing imminent death—revealed "his soul," his true identity as Nichiren the Buddha. This described his "casting off the transient and revealing the true."

ATTAINING ENLIGHTENMENT AS AN ORDINARY PERSON

Of course, when Nichiren "cast off" his transient status as an ordinary person, he didn't stop being an ordinary person or become some sort of transcendent being. Rather, while remaining an ordinary person, he revealed the eternal Buddha nature that already existed in his life, exemplifying that there is no Buddha apart from ordinary human beings.

To "cast off the transient" is like opening up or removing the clouds that block the sun's light.[2] We cast off the "transient" clouds of delusion, karma, and suffering by bringing forth the same wisdom, courage, and compassion that Nichiren demonstrated.

Nichiren's commitment to kosen-rufu—to awaken all people to their inherent enlightenment, no matter the obstacles or circumstances—enabled him to reveal the brightest sun of Buddhahood.

He writes, "Here a single individual has been used as an example, but the same thing applies equally to all living beings" (WND-2, 844). In other words, Nichiren's "casting off the transient and revealing the true" opened the path for all of us to attain Buddhahood.

"REVEALING THE TRUE" EACH DAY

The source of Nichiren's enlightenment was his vow to realize kosen-rufu.

President Ikeda reminds us: "The heart of the great vow for kosen-rufu and the life state of Buddhahood are one and the same. Therefore, when we dedicate our lives to this vow, we can bring forth the supreme nobility, strength, and greatness of our lives."[3]

To emphasize this point, Nichiren inscribed the Gohonzon, a crystallization of that highest state of life.

Therefore, every day when we chant Nam-myoho-renge-kyo to the Gohonzon, we "cast off the transient and reveal the true" in our own lives.

President Ikeda clarifies what this means for us:

> There is no impasse we cannot break through with faith in the Mystic Law. There is no need to give up or be discouraged in the face of difficulty. Instead, serenely laugh off your troubles! Cause the invincible spirit of Soka to blaze up and burn bright. Rouse the great power of faith and practice, chanting Nam-myoho-renge-kyo and taking action. It is by challenging ourselves in our human revolution in this way that we "cast off the transient and reveal the true" in our own lives.[4]

As we chant to the Gohonzon, study Nichiren's writings, and share Buddhism with others, we can "cast off " the barriers of cowardice, selfishness, and doubt. And we can open up boundless courage, generosity, and confidence within, wisely surmounting one obstacle after another as we proudly proclaim: "What greater joy could there be?"

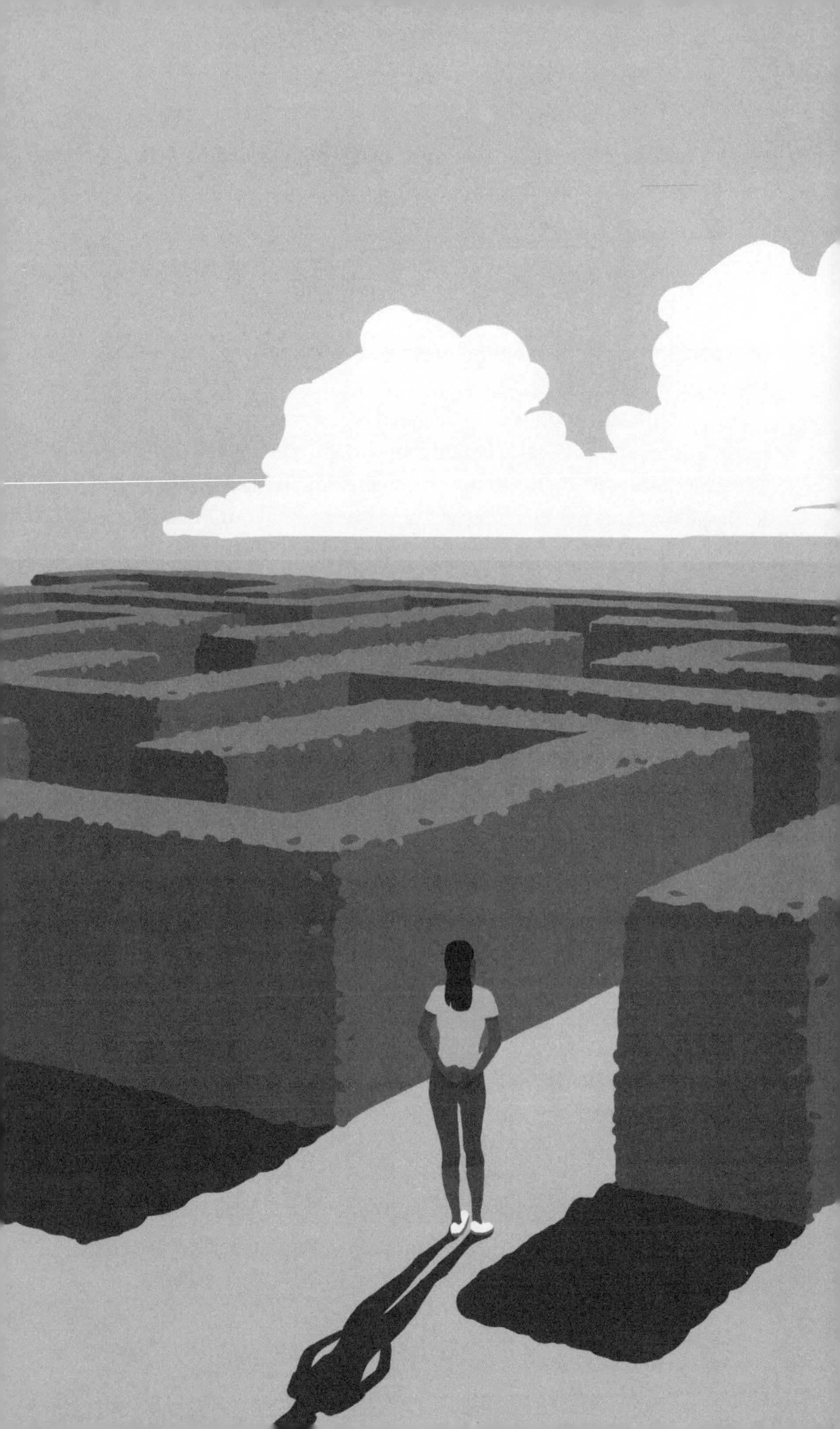

CONCEPT ELEVEN

CHANGING KARMA
Outshining Our Karma With the "Sun of Wisdom"

What have I done to deserve this? We've probably all asked ourselves this question, especially when facing problems that don't make sense to us.

Buddhism explains that karma has a lot to do with why we find ourselves in our present circumstances.

While there's good, bad, and even neutral karma, people often associate karma with negative or bad outcomes. This might be because human beings tend to take the good things in life for granted and take particular note of the bad.

Going beyond such perceptions, Nichiren Buddhism offers a liberating and empowering understanding of karma.

But first, let's take a look at how the idea of karma has evolved.

KARMA MEANS "ACTION"

In brief, the Sanskrit word *karma* means "to act" or "action." We take action in three ways: through our thoughts, speech, and behavior. And our moment-to-moment actions, or causes, remain dormant in our lives as "latent effects" that will eventually manifest when the conditions are right. Our cumulative actions from previous lifetimes determine our present circumstances and personal characteristics.

Predating Buddhism, the idea of karma existed in ancient India but almost as an absolute. People were compelled to accept the conditions they were born into or the misfortunes they met with as their "karma." This understanding of karma comes close to the concept of "fate" or "destiny."

Later, Shakyamuni Buddha taught that our fate is not predetermined; instead, by striving to take the best actions in the present, we can lead the best life in the future. In addition, the influence of our actions transcends life and death and is carried on into future existences.

Ultimately, based on the Lotus Sutra, Nichiren Daishonin taught that because each of us possesses the Buddha nature, we have the inherent power to free ourselves from the chains of karma in this life and beyond.

CHANTING AND SPREADING THE MYSTIC LAW: THE GREATEST GOOD CAUSE

After Shakyamuni's passing, most Buddhists recognized only a general view of causality. They regarded cause and effect as purely sequential—good causes yield similar good effects while bad causes produce similar bad effects. Based on this view alone, however, it would require lifetimes or eons of intensive practice to cancel out all bad causes from the past and accumulate enough good ones to attain Buddhahood. One would also have to refrain from making any new negative causes, a nearly impossible feat.

In contrast to this general view of causality, Nichiren Daishonin makes a revolutionary statement: "My sufferings . . . are not ascribable to this causal law" (WND-1, 305).

He clarifies that the deepest negative cause is slandering the Lotus Sutra, or the Mystic Law of the universe. It is to disregard the sutra's central principle—that all people inherently possess Buddhahood and are equally worthy of respect. To slander the Lotus Sutra, then, means to denigrate or deny our own and others' true potential and dignity. It represents the ultimate form of evil and creates the gravest negative causes.

In contrast, the greatest good cause we can make is to revere the Mystic Law that is the essence of all people's lives. It is to awaken our Buddha nature and help others do the same.

Rather than accumulating minor good causes for lifetimes or eons to do so, we can achieve that awakening right now: we can bring forth the "sun" of our Buddha nature the moment we chant Nam-myoho-renge-kyo to the Gohonzon. This is known as "the simultaneity of cause and effect."

A passage in the Lotus Sutra states, "The host of sins, like frost or dew, can be wiped out by the sun of wisdom" (LSOC, 390).

Commenting on this, Nichiren says:

> The "host of sins" are karmic impediments that come from the six sense organs,[1] and these are like frost or dew. Thus, although they exist, they can be wiped out by the sun of wisdom. The "sun of wisdom" is Nam-myoho-renge-kyo, which Nichiren is propagating now in the Latter Day of the Law. (OTT, 205)

By chanting and sharing the practice of Nam-myoho-renge-kyo, the greatest good, we can bring forth the "sun of wisdom" in our lives. President Ikeda explains:

> Just as the light of the stars and the moon seems to vanish when the sun rises, when we bring forth the state of Buddhahood in our lives we cease to suffer negative effects for each individual past offense committed.
>
> In other words, this does not deny or contradict general causality. General causality remains an underlying premise of Buddhism. But it is subsumed by what might be termed a "greater causality." This greater causality is the causality of

attaining Buddhahood. It is the causality of the Lotus Sutra and the Mystic Law.[2]

So while our karma doesn't just magically disappear, rather than suffer on account of our karma, we can use it to prove the power of our lives and overcome any and all obstacles. The negative influence of our bad karma pales in comparison to the brilliance of our state of life.

OUR KARMA IS OUR MISSION

Let's take this one step further toward full self-empowerment.

By elevating our lives and facing difficulties head-on, we can inspire countless others. It is through winning over hardships that we prove the power of our Buddhist practice and open the way for all others to awaken to their Buddhahood.

President Ikeda once encouraged a woman who had lost her husband and was left to raise her young children alone, saying:

> By regaining vitality and good health, someone who has been battling illness can light a flame of courage in the hearts of those in similar straits. By creating a happy and harmonious family, a person who has suffered great anguish over discord in the home can become a model for others plagued by family problems.
>
> Similarly, if you—a woman who has been left widowed in a foreign land where she does not speak the language—become happy and raise your children to be fine adults, you'll be a shining example for all women who have lost their partners. Even those who don't practice Nichiren Buddhism will admire you and come to seek your advice.
>
> So you see, the deeper and greater the suffering, the more magnificently one can show proof of the powerful benefit of Buddhism.[3]

By developing our lives through our Buddhist practice and sharing the Buddhist ideal of respect for the dignity of all life, we not only free ourselves from the karmic cycle of suffering, we can turn our karma into our mission, opening the way for many others, for all of humanity, to do the same.

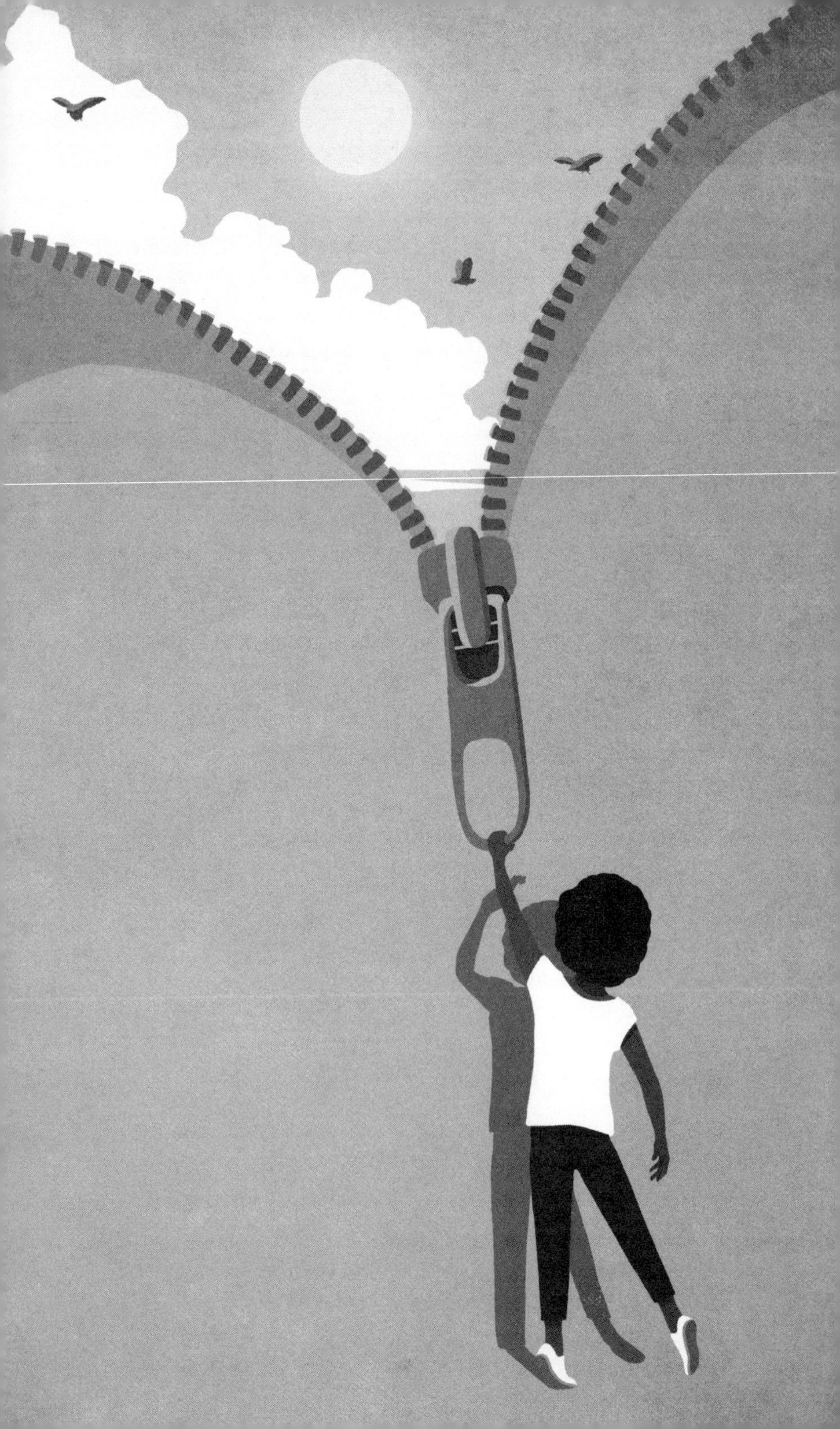

CONCEPT TWELVE

THE MUTUAL POSSESSION OF THE TEN WORLDS
Every Situation Is the Best Situation for Elevating Our Lives

We all experience various situations each day. At times, we respond in ways that highlight our wonderful character, other times, not so much: we might do or say something we regret or that causes us to suffer. We could spend hours caring for a friend in need but then that same day get into a heated argument with our partner and say mean, hurtful words.

Despite such shifts in how we deal with things, each of us is an infinitely precious and noble Buddha who possesses limitless reserves of courage, wisdom, and compassion.

Having conviction in this is difficult, however. Nichiren Daishonin says: "We ordinary people can see neither our own eyelashes, which are so close, nor the heavens in the distance. Likewise, we do not see that the Buddha exists in our own hearts" (WND-1, 1137).

So let's learn from the concept of the mutual possession of the Ten Worlds, which offers insights into how we can not only believe in our Buddhahood but bring it forth anytime, anywhere.

THE MEANING OF "MUTUAL POSSESSION"

The concept of the Ten Worlds teaches that we can experience at any moment any of the ten states of life that are potential within us, ranging from the lowest world of hell to the highest world of Buddhahood.[1] We manifest any one of these Ten Worlds at each given moment, the other nine remaining latent.

This process is not linear or fixed. We jump around from one state of life to another throughout the day, moment to moment, based on various internal and external conditions.

Here, "mutual possession" of these ten states of life means that each world contains the potential for all ten. The point? Each state of life exists in the world of Buddhahood, and Buddhahood exists within each world.

This means that Buddhas remain ordinary people and will still experience various life states. It also means that we can tap our inner Buddhahood no matter what state of life we're in.

So, how do we do this?

We can instantly access Buddhahood by chanting Nam-myoho-renge-kyo. Through chanting, we elevate our life condition and bring forth our Buddha nature. Rather than being controlled by our baser instincts, we can muster the courage to face anything, bring forth the greatest wisdom and compassion, and create utmost value right where we are.

Moreover, because we've accumulated countless causes from past lifetimes, we default to one of the Ten Worlds. For instance, we might tend to respond with anger in certain situations (*asuras*) or feel that we never have enough of whatever it is we want (hungry spirits).

But through our practice of Buddhism, we can make Buddhahood our default, our basic life tendency. This means that, even though we still have worries (other nine worlds), our lives operate based on ever-increasing joy, wisdom, compassion, and courage (Buddhahood).

We can bring forth our Buddhahood by chanting and doing gongyo every day, studying Buddhism, sharing it with others, and making the happiness of ourselves and others the motivation for everything we do.

THE MINDSET OF A BUDDHA: EACH CHALLENGE IS AN OPPORTUNITY

Describing a Buddha as "one who embodies the mutual possession of the Ten Worlds," President Ikeda says:

> The world of Buddhahood can also be described as a state of life where one willingly takes on even hellish suffering. This is the world of hell contained in the world of Buddhahood. It is characterized by empathy and hardships deliberately taken on for the happiness and welfare of others, and it arises from a sense of responsibility and compassion. Courageously taking on problems and sufferings for the sake of others strengthens the world of Buddhahood in our lives.[2]

Based on the mutual possession of the Ten Worlds, everything we go through becomes raw material for fortifying our Buddhahood and for encouraging and awakening others to their inherent power. By changing our default through continued Buddhist practice, we can come to use each experience, negative or positive, to generate even more happiness.

In the midst of an argument, a devastating loss, or a debilitating illness, we may not always see where the happiness will come from. But continually striving to live in this way enables us to establish the unshakable life state of Buddhahood.

Will we see our challenges as setbacks and causes for suffering? Or as opportunities to strengthen and enrich our lives? Knowing that our Buddhahood is always accessible or right around the corner helps us live with complete peace of mind, using everything to advance our happiness.

And as we strive each day to elevate our basic life tendencies and urge others to do the same, the state of our society will likewise transform and move toward Buddhahood.

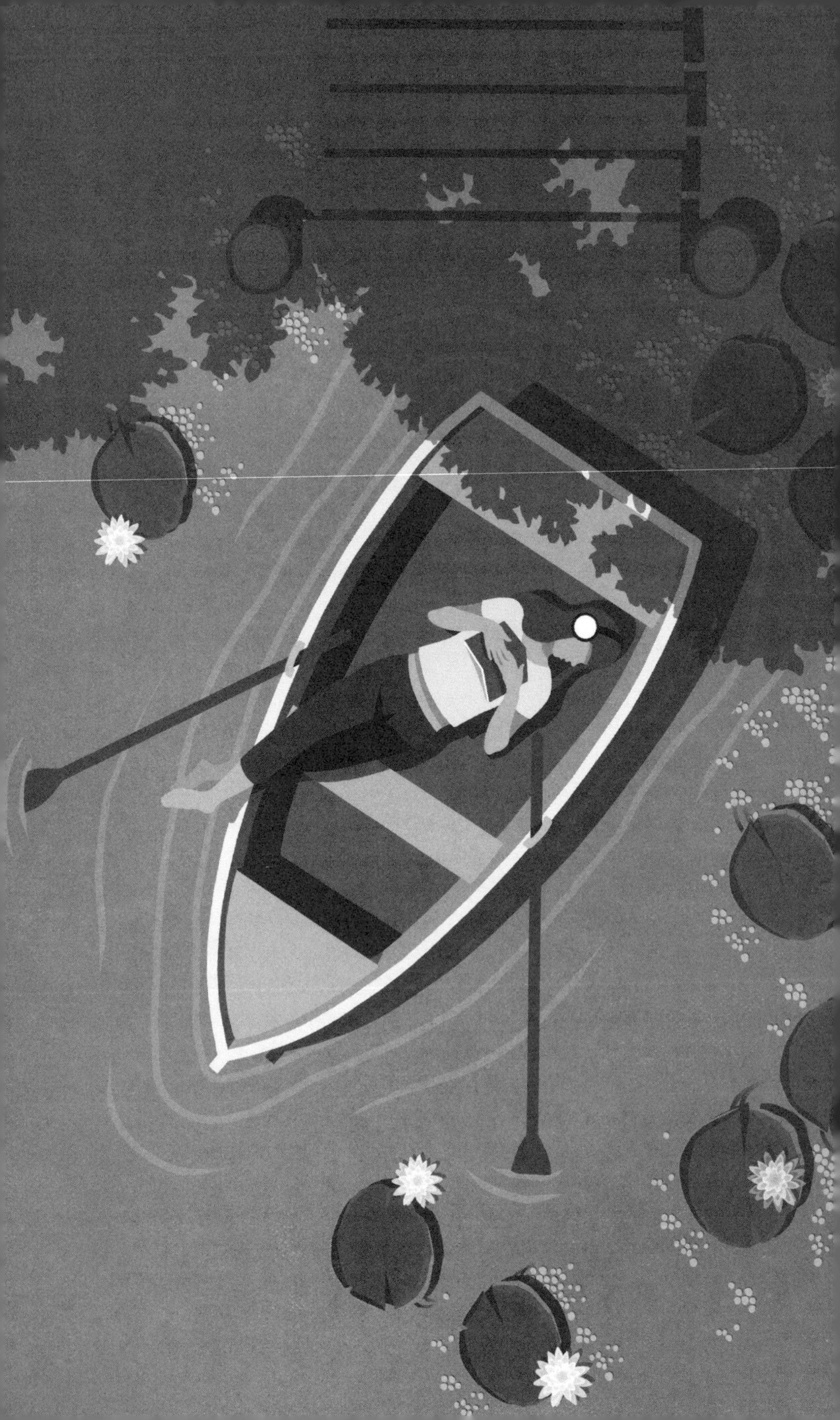

THREE THOUSAND REALMS IN A SINGLE MOMENT OF LIFE
Tap Your Greatest Potential at Any Moment

Each instant of life contains incredible possibilities. Most important among these, especially when facing problems, is our ability to bring forth the strength and resolve to win—to forge ahead with hope, joy, and courage while challenging our doubts or fears. Such inner resolve, Buddhism teaches, is the key to a happy, fulfilling life.

Countless Soka Gakkai members have demonstrated this by using their Buddhist practice to overcome all kinds of challenges, reaching goals they thought were unreachable and creating a solid foundation for lasting happiness.

A core principle in Nichiren Buddhism is three thousand realms in a single moment of life, which describes why this is possible. Nichiren Daishonin uses it to teach that a change in our inner resolve can change everything.

Today, we face endless uncertainties, including worries about the coronavirus pandemic, issues with relationships, finances, or social division. Nevertheless, we can shape the life we envision and positively affect those around us by chanting Nam-myoho-renge-kyo to the Gohonzon. By practicing and sharing Buddhism, and refreshing our resolve to win in any situation, we become stronger, wiser, and more understanding of ourselves and others.

President Ikeda says:

> This principle [of three thousand realms in a single moment of life] holds that each life-moment is endowed with three thousand different functions, which influence not only our own lives but those of all around us; they also influence society, our natural environment, and the earth. They encompass the entire universe.
>
> Therefore, once you have decided to do something, the three thousand functions and your entire being start working to help you reach your goal. The entire universe also starts moving toward the fulfillment of your goal. If you pray "This is how I want to be," and continue to work toward your dream, you will gradually realize the future you have envisaged.[1]

The concepts behind three thousand realms in a single moment of life are profound and complex and difficult to explain fully in this brief chapter. But they describe the incredible potential and power our lives possess. That said, hopefully, the overview that follows sheds a little light on this principle.

WHERE DOES THE NUMBER THREE THOUSAND COME FROM?

The Great Teacher T'ien-t'ai[2] in the sixth century developed the principle of three thousand realms in a single moment of life as a way to explain the truth revealed in the Lotus Sutra: that the tremendous potential called Buddhahood resides in each person's life.

"Three thousand realms" points to all aspects of life and their varied functions, while "a single moment of life" refers to life at any moment.

The number three thousand combines three Buddhist concepts that approach life and the law of causality from different perspectives. It derives from multiplying the number one hundred—from the mutual possession of the Ten Worlds (ten worlds times ten worlds equals one hundred)—by the "ten factors of life" and then by the "three realms of existence" (one hundred times ten times three equals three thousand).

THE MUTUAL POSSESSION OF THE TEN WORLDS

"The doctrine of three thousand realms in a single moment of life," Nichiren says, "begins with the concept of the mutual possession of the Ten Worlds" (WND-1, 224), which, as explained in the previous chapter, shows that the nine worlds exist within the world of Buddhahood and that the world of Buddhahood is inherent and can be expressed only within the reality of the other nine worlds.

This concept clarifies the Lotus Sutra's teaching that all living beings fundamentally possess Buddhahood, the most enlightened state of life, and that we can bring it forth at any time by chanting Nam-myoho-renge-kyo.

THE TEN FACTORS OF LIFE

While the Ten Worlds describe different ways we experience life, the ten factors of life describe how the life state we are in—any of the Ten Worlds—is expressed at each moment in our life and environment.

Every day in the first section of our recitation of the Lotus Sutra, Nichiren Buddhists repeat three times these ten factors from the second chapter, "Expedient Means." They are: (1) appearance, (2) nature, (3) entity, (4) power, (5) influence, (6) internal cause, (7) relation, (8) latent effect, (9) manifest effect, and (10) consistency from beginning to end.[3]

The first three factors describe the essence of a living being, while the next six describe the law of cause and effect, or how the Ten Worlds manifest in our lives. The last factor, "consistency from beginning to end," indicates that all nine factors are consistent for each of the Ten Worlds.

For example, when we are in the world of hell, it shows on our face, we see people and situations through that lens, and we act out of frustration or rage.

Likewise, because we possess the potential for Buddhahood, when we attend SGI meetings, study, chant, or tell others about Buddhism, that sparks the "internal cause" for us to experience and express in all aspects of our lives the workings of the world of Buddhahood.

THE THREE REALMS OF EXISTENCE

Finally, a transformation in our core mindset transforms the three realms of existence, which are three different standpoints of life: (1) the realm of the five components[4] (the individual), (2) the realm of living beings (society), and (3) the realm of the environment (the environment in which we live).

These three realms represent our actual world and are not separate. Instead, they are parts of an integrated whole in which any of the Ten Worlds can manifest. They describe everything we each have to deal with—ourselves, our relationships with others, and our environment.

Just as Nichiren emphasizes that "it is the heart that is important" (WND-1, 1000), the first of these three realms, which represents the inner workings of life, is key. When the state of our heart and mind changes, it effects a change in our interactions with those around us and our environment.

A SIMPLE, EFFECTIVE APPROACH

Nichiren Daishonin took the profound and comprehensive view that is three thousand realms in a single moment of life and engineered a simple way to apply it to our daily lives so that we can bring forth our Buddhahood, just as he did.

He explains that the benefits possessed by all Buddhas and inherent in all Buddhist sutras, the Lotus in particular, are fully contained within Nam-myoho-renge-kyo. It is the Law, the seed of Buddhahood, by which ordinary people can realize enlightenment.

He manifested in his own life as an ordinary person this Law for attaining Buddhahood and embodied it in substantial ways—in his words and behavior.

He then crystallized that state of life directly in the form of the Gohonzon, which we regard as the concrete expression of three thousand realms in a single moment of life.

And today, through our practice of chanting Nam-myoho-renge-kyo to the Gohonzon—even without fully grasping the principle of three thousand realms in a single moment of life—we can draw forth limitless courage, hope, and resilience to surmount challenges and make the impossible possible.

President Ikeda says:

> When we chant before the Gohonzon, we can perceive the true nature of our lives and manifest the world of Buddhahood.
> Our attitude or determination in faith is perfectly reflected in the mirror of the Gohonzon and mirrored in the universe. This accords with the principle of three thousand realms in a single moment of life. . . .
> Accordingly, our attitude or mind is extremely important. Our deep-seated attitude or determination in faith has a subtle and far-reaching influence.[5]

Through powerful prayer to the Gohonzon, we can tap our greatest potential at any moment and share the joy and freedom it gives us with our families, communities, and society, and ultimately transform the entire world.

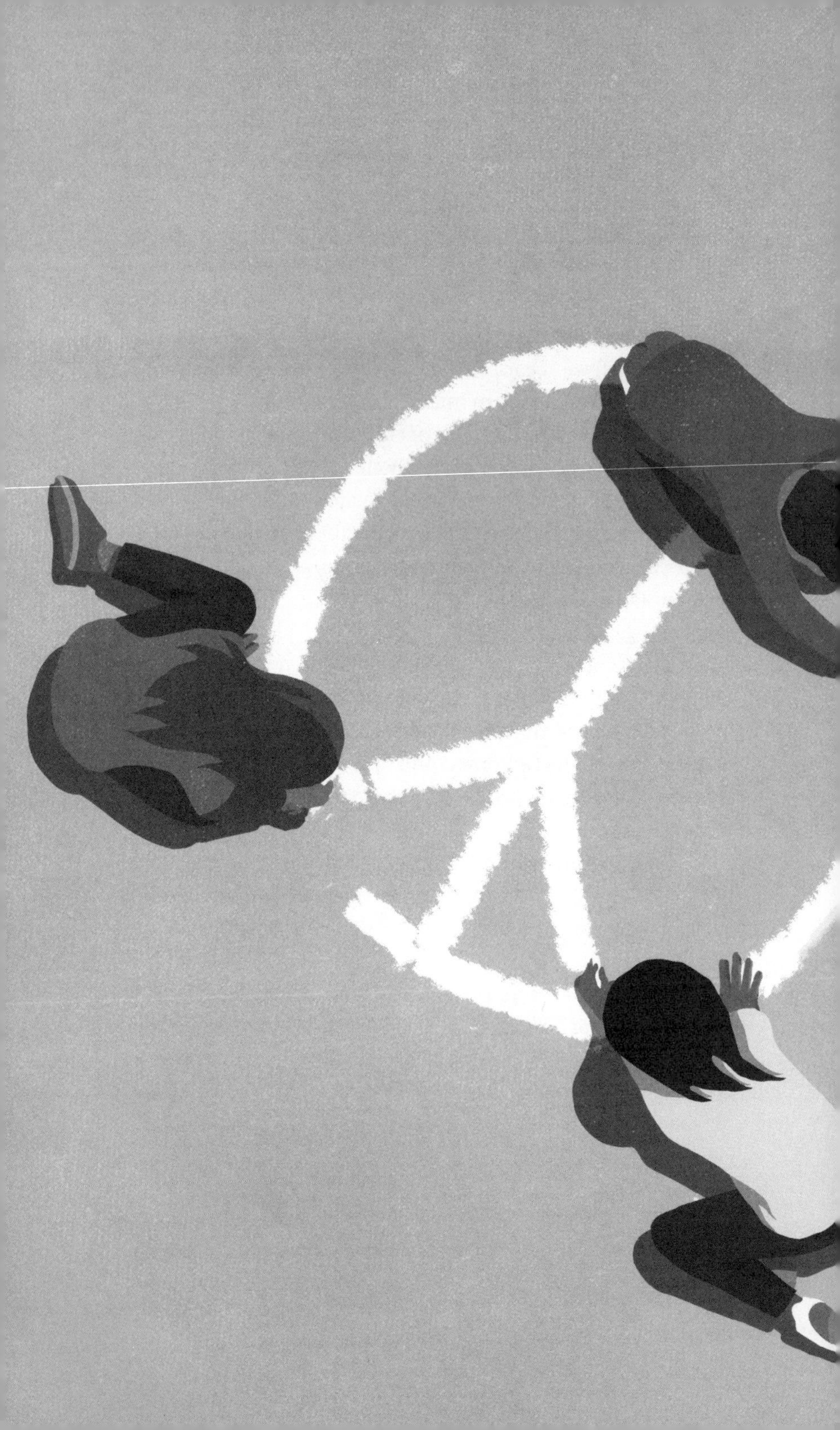

CONCEPT FOURTEEN

MANY IN BODY, ONE IN MIND
Unity in Diversity

In the world today, we can see countless examples of discord and lack of respect—from bullying online, at school, and work to intensifying political divisions that cause people to dismiss or vilify those on the opposing side.

Whether in our personal relationships or society at large, difficulty cooperating with others is at the core of many problems we face.

While we often hear calls for unity and understanding from commentators in many fields, Nichiren Daishonin offers a unique approach through the principle of many in body, one in mind. He writes:

> All disciples and lay supporters of Nichiren should chant Nam-myoho-renge-kyo with the spirit of many in body but one in mind, transcending all differences among themselves to become as inseparable as fish and the water in which they swim. This spiritual bond is the basis for the universal transmission of the ultimate Law of life and death. Herein lies the true goal of Nichiren's propagation. (WND-1, 217)

The Daishonin established the practice of chanting Nam-myoho-renge-kyo, the ultimate Law of the universe, to enable all people to lead lives of absolute happiness. And he taught that chanting with the united spirit of "many in body, one in mind" is crucial in this endeavor.

"Many in body" refers to each person's unique opinions, backgrounds, abilities, and roles—it means respect for diversity and individuality. As practitioners of Nichiren Buddhism, being "one in mind" means taking Nichiren's vow to spread the Law for people's happiness as one's own mission and working toward its realization.

Simply put, uniting for the noblest cause of awakening people to their ability to become truly happy connects directly to creating a peaceful world. In practical terms, it means that we, as Buddhists, have a mission to engender trust, respect, empathy, and understanding among those around us. Through our resolve to work together in unity for the sake of kosen-rufu, we gain the ability to create harmony in our homes, workplaces, and communities.

GENUINE UNITY HIGHLIGHTS EACH PERSON'S UNIQUENESS

Unity, however, doesn't mean conformity or denying our differences. Rather, Nichiren Buddhism emphasizes the importance of "transcending differences," overcoming the antagonism that arises from such differences—feelings such as contempt, jealousy, resentment, arrogance, malice, ingratitude, and the like. Identifying and chanting Nam-myoho-renge-kyo to rise above such tendencies enables us to develop respect even for those with whom we don't agree.

President Ikeda notes that "many in body, one in mind" signals "unity in diversity:"[1]

> Though we may share the same purpose or aspiration, we do not suppress or deny our own individuality. When we each fully express our unique potential through the power of the

Mystic Law, we can manifest the invincible strength of the unity of many in body, one in mind.[2]

From this perspective, striving to create unity is what allows each of us to exhibit our unique strengths while pooling those strengths to bring even the loftiest of goals within reach.

UNITY STARTS WITH OURSELVES

What if we don't see such unity?

President Ikeda says, "Everything begins with changing our own attitude, or mindset."[3] In other words, unity starts with us. Just one person deciding to elevate themselves is key to creating harmonious relationships.

When we don't see eye to eye with someone, we can: (1) chant Nam-myoho-renge-kyo; (2) refresh our resolve to be the one who creates unity; (3) engage others with a willingness to listen to their point of view; (4) find points of agreement. By repeating the process of chanting, taking action, and reflecting, we can find the best way forward.

Regarding the significance of creating unity, the Daishonin writes, "Herein lies the true goal of Nichiren's propagation." Therefore, it's vital to understand that our efforts to unite with our fellow SGI members for the sake of kosen-rufu enhance our ability to create harmony with anyone, anywhere.

Amid the divisiveness and angst of today's society, when we mend the discord and lack of respect in our own lives as well as with those around us, we bring the world one step closer to the harmony and respect it so desperately needs.

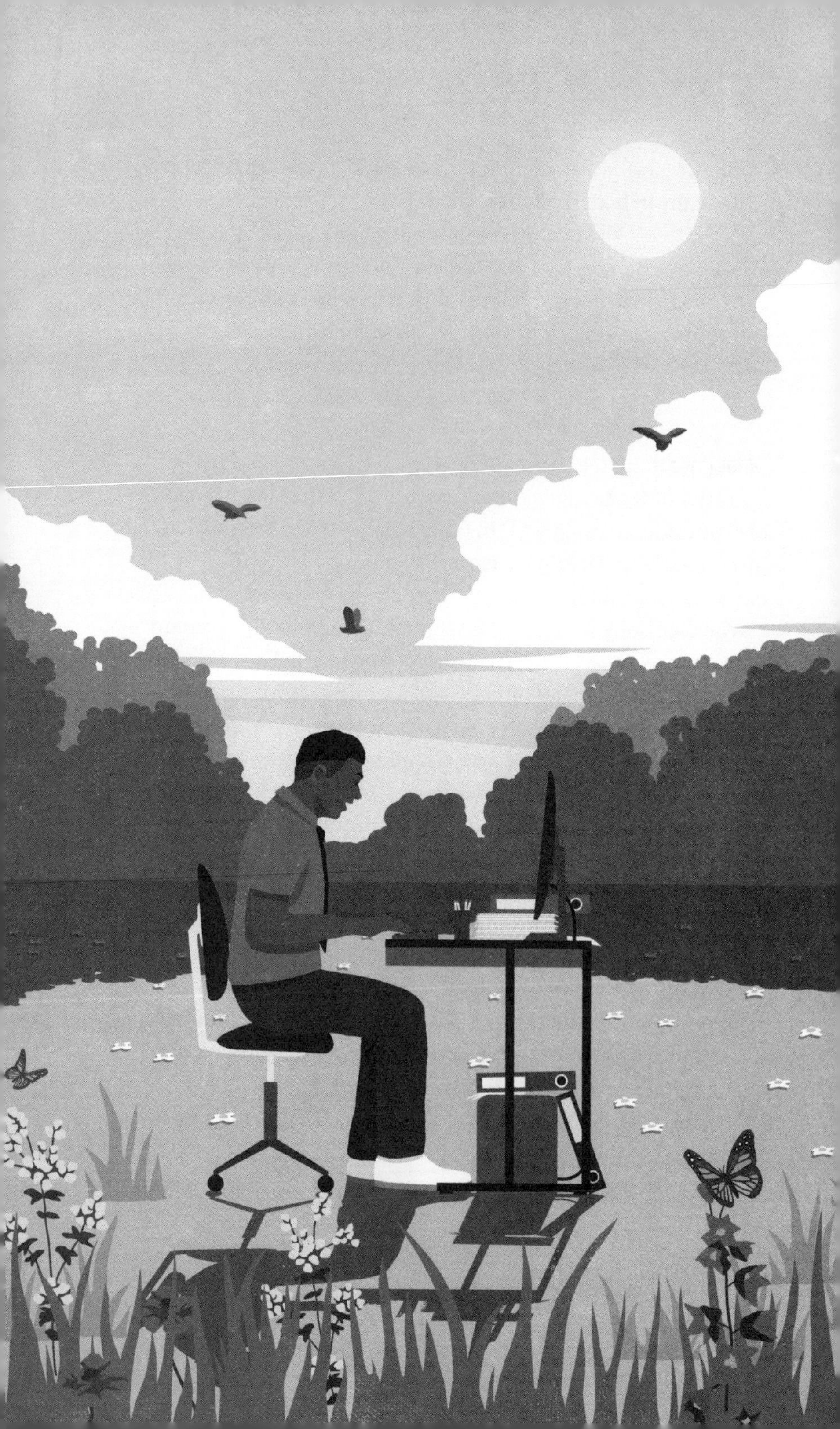

CONCEPT FIFTEEN

FAITH EQUALS DAILY LIFE
The Power to Win Each Day

We may dream of being happy one day, that sometime in the future we will have everything we want and be problem free.

But Buddhism teaches that we can be happy right now, even amid all the stresses of daily life.

A key idea in Nichiren Buddhism that points to how to experience such happiness is "faith equals daily life." Many think religion and daily life occupy separate spaces. But Nichiren Daishonin says, "A person of wisdom is not one who practices Buddhism apart from worldly affairs but, rather, one who thoroughly understands the principles by which the world is governed" (WND-1, 1121).

As this passage reveals, "a person of wisdom" understands that daily life is the exact place for carrying out our Buddhist practice and that our attitude and actions each day express our faith.

Chanting Nam-myoho-renge-kyo to the Gohonzon and bringing forth our Buddhahood help us rise to the challenge that each day brings. As we continue to do so, we come to understand our personal strengths. We learn how to transform difficulties with others and create respectful, harmonious relationships.

UPHOLDING DILIGENT FAITH

We may easily relate to Shijo Kingo, one of Nichiren Daishonin's trusted disciples. His story illustrates how to create happiness based on the principle of faith equals daily life. He was on track to success in his multifaceted career as a samurai, physician, and estate manager. Yet he often ran into problems with his coworkers and siblings, and sometimes even with fellow Buddhists, mostly due to his sense of righteousness and quick temper. His most redeeming quality was his devotion to Nichiren and his teaching.

At one point, he urged his feudal lord, Ema Mitsutoki, to embrace the Daishonin's teaching. This led Ema, who was influenced by a priest who hated Nichiren and by rumors spread by Kingo's jealous colleagues, to threaten to confiscate Kingo's estates if he didn't recant his faith in the Lotus Sutra.

Though distressed, Kingo challenged himself each day to follow Nichiren's instruction—to remain calm and loyal to his lord, while also trusting and upholding his faith in the Lotus Sutra.

Eventually, when Lord Ema suddenly fell ill, Kingo was there to treat him and help him recover, and he regained Ema's trust. By applying faith to his daily life, he'd won.

In June 1277, as Kingo's situation improved, Nichiren wrote to him:

> Life as a human being is hard to sustain—as hard as it is for the dew to remain on the grass. But it is better to live a single day with honor than to live to 120 and die in disgrace. Live so that all the people of Kamakura will say in your praise that Nakatsukasa Saburo Saemon-no-jo [Shijo Kingo] is diligent in the service of his lord, in the service of Buddhism, and in his concern for other people. (WND-1, 851)

More important than how long we live is how we live each day with a sense of fulfillment and purpose.

In the end, Kingo learned the importance of building trust and turned his entire situation around.

THREE POINTS FOR LIVING A FULFILLING DAILY LIFE

Based on the passage above, President Ikeda offers three key points for finding happiness in our daily realities:

1. *Build trust with those around us*: "'In the service of one's lord,' . . . means building a solid relationship of trust with one's boss or employer. It means becoming an outstanding employee at our workplace or excelling in our profession. It also refers to our behavior as members of society."

2. *Consistently strengthen our Buddhist practice*: "'In the service of Buddhism' means to practice steadfastly, always basing ourselves on faith in the Mystic Law."

3. *Extend ourselves to others*: "'In concern for other people' means caring qualities, like a sincere interest in others, that earn the respect and trust of those around us as we live our lives in society."[1]

As we cultivate these three qualities and our ability to better navigate our daily lives, we become "people of wisdom." The more we strengthen our foundation in faith, the more we become adept at using everything that happens each day to propel our own happiness and help those around us excel in their lives.

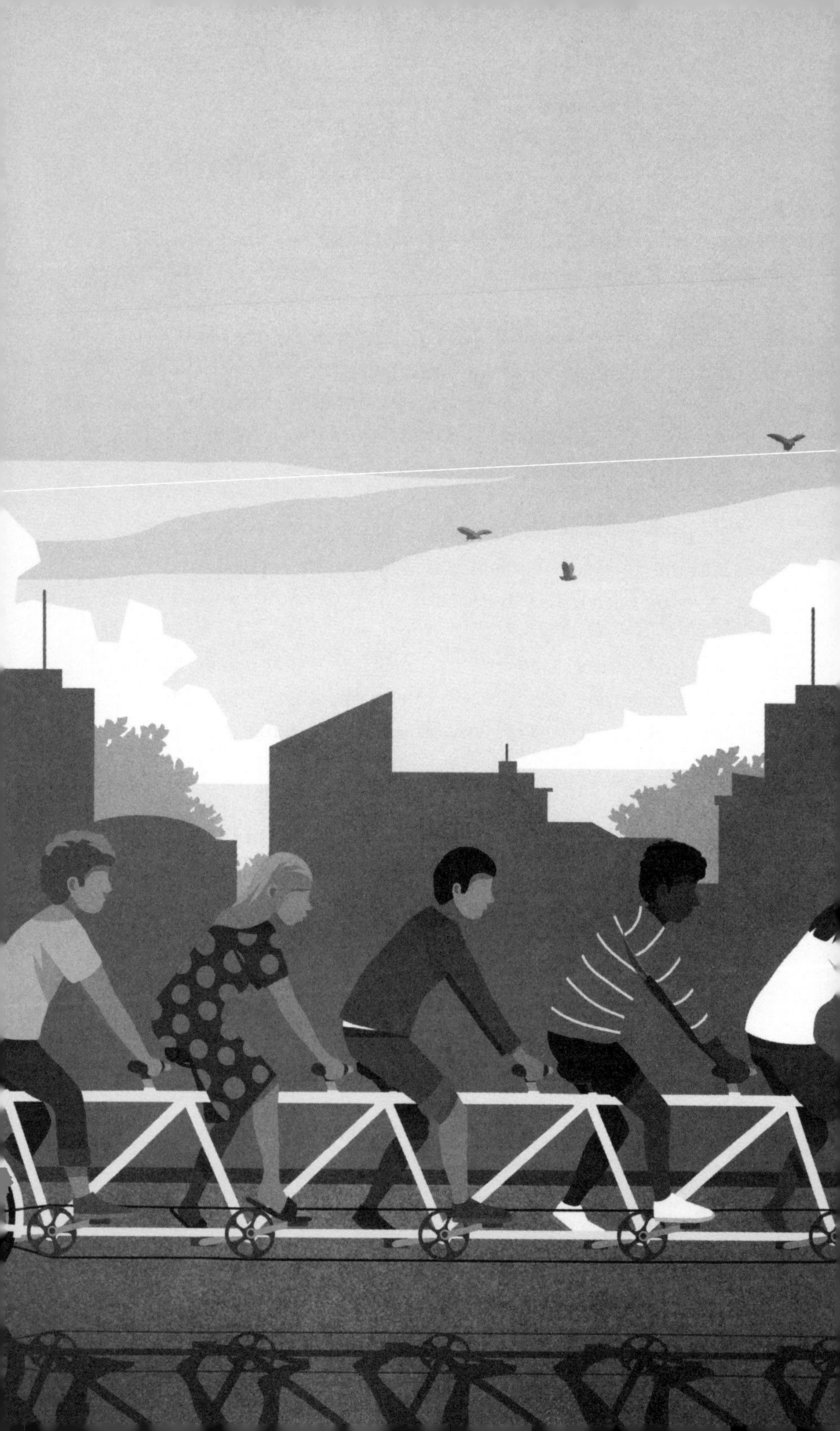

CONCEPT SIXTEEN

ONENESS
We Are Connected to Everyone, Everything

What did the Buddhist say to the hot dog vendor? "Make me one with everything."

You've probably heard this joke, but that most laugh at it shows how people generally associate the idea of "oneness" with Buddhism.

Nevertheless, it's probably safe to assume that few people think too long or hard about being one with everything around them. It may seem idealistic, symbolic of new-age or counterculture thinking with no practical application.

From the Buddhist perspective, however, oneness is a revolutionary yet superbly practical idea.

The Oneness Hypothesis brings together essays looking at oneness from philosophical, religious, and psychological perspectives. The book jacket reads: "Oneness provides ways to imagine and achieve a more expansive conception of the self as fundamentally connected with other people, creatures, and things. Such views present profound challenges to Western hyperindividualism and its excessive concern with self-interest and tendency toward self-centered behavior."[1]

Challenging as it may be, this notion of oneness offers a way toward discovering a greater, more profound sense of happiness for individuals as well as for society as a whole.

GROWING SCIENTIFIC EVIDENCE POINTS TO THE INTERRELATEDNESS OF ALL THINGS

Concerns about the increasing division and polarization in the world today is prompting many to more deeply consider our commonalities as fellow human beings and seek a way to create something positive out of contrasting or opposing ideas and forces.

Over the past century, science has proven connections between many disparate ideas and phenomena where no connection was seen before.

We now know that body and mind, long assumed to be separate, are interrelated on a subatomic level, two functions of the same living system.

Likewise, we recognize that human life and the natural environment are so interdependent that we can no longer afford to regard them as separate.

More than a hundred years ago, physicists described the mysterious relationship between matter and energy, showing that light, for instance, behaves as both a particle and a wave. Just before that, Albert Einstein described with a simple equation the intrinsic, interchangeable relationship between matter, time, space, and energy.

In this series, through our study of "three thousand realms in a single moment of life," we've seen that life at any instant possesses the potential of the entire universe while at the same time permeating the entire universe.

THE TEN ONENESSES AND MORE!

The Great Teacher Miao-lo,[2] drawing from the teachings of the Lotus Sutra, introduced the idea of "ten onenesses."

They are: (1) the oneness of body and mind; (2) the oneness of the internal and the external; (3) the oneness of the result of practice and the true nature of life; (4) the oneness of cause and effect; (5) the oneness of the impure and the pure; (6) the oneness of life and its environment; (7) the oneness of self and others; (8) the oneness of thought, word, and deed; (9) the oneness of the provisional and true teachings; and (10) the oneness of benefits.[3]

Explaining the implications of all ten would require a book that few would ever read. Perhaps this is why President Ikeda says:

> We may simply note that the point of [this] doctrine is that terms which appear to be opposites, such as body and mind or pure and impure, can be viewed as a single entity. Thus, for example, considered from a general point of view, body and mind constitute a single concept, though when they are considered from a specific point of view they can be broken down into the two categories of body and mind.[4]

And while *oneness* is a convenient English word, the Japanese term describing these relationships is *funi*, literally meaning "not two," a contraction of the phrase *nini-funi*, or "two but not two."

From this, we can see that oneness doesn't deny distinctions between two contrasting ideas, entities, or principles. Rather, it asserts that, while different, neither can be considered independent of the other. Both arise from the same source, the Law that underlies life itself: Nam-myoho-renge-kyo.

In addition to these ten, Nichiren Buddhism posits other onenesses, including the oneness of good and evil and the oneness of mentor and disciple.

Closely related to "two but not two" is the word *soku* in Japanese, often translated as "equals," "is," or "manifests."

Terms using this word suggest that distinct ideas are inextricable. As President Ikeda says:

> Buddhism teaches the profound concept of simultaneity,

oneness, or nonduality (or *soku* in Japanese). It is central to such principles as "earthly desires are (*soku*) enlightenment," "the sufferings of birth and death are (*soku*) nirvana." . . . This, however, is not merely a linking together of two opposing elements—for instance, delusion and enlightenment—with an equal sign. It actually conveys a dynamic relationship between them, a springboard, a trigger, or a vector from the first element to the next—for example, delusion functioning as the springboard to enlightenment. As such, it is an important concept in terms of our actual Buddhist practice and also represents a philosophy of supreme hope.

No matter what obstacles or hardships we may encounter in our efforts to achieve kosen-rufu based on faith, we can definitely surmount them. We should have the unshakable conviction that difficulties are actually opportunities in that they give us a chance to change our karma and build a solid foundation for victory in our lives. And we should keep moving forward with courageous faith based on that conviction, staying on the path to absolute victory, the path of the Mystic Law.[5]

The next few chapters will explore life-changing principles based on oneness: the oneness of body and mind; the oneness of good and evil; the oneness of life and environment; and the oneness of mentor and disciple.

Ultimately, the principle that unites each pair is the Mystic Law itself, Nam-myoho-renge-kyo, our practice of which enables us to create the greatest value from their connection.

By studying these together, we can gain deeper insight into Buddhist faith and practice, and its applicability to every aspect of life, both for individuals and for society.

CONCEPT SEVENTEEN

ONENESS OF BODY AND MIND
Our Resolve Is Everything

We have learned more about the brain in the last ten years than in any previous century.[1] And although body and mind were previously thought to be separate and distinct, science and medicine have proven their close interrelatedness, or inseparability. How we think largely affects how we feel, both physically and emotionally.

For instance, many studies show that stress can cause stomachaches and impact our gut health.[2] Some research also links listening to music to lowering blood pressure and positively affecting other cardiovascular functions.[3]

Buddhism also teaches the interrelatedness of our bodies and minds, and how to fundamentally transform our lives based on the principle of the oneness of body and mind, or *shikishin-funi* in Japanese.

Shiki literally means "color," "hue," or "appearance" and refers to physical existence. *Shin* means "mind" or "heart" and refers to spiritual or intangible attributes. And *funi* is a truncation of the phrase *nini-funi*, which means "two but not two," connoting the inseparability of the physical and spiritual aspects of life.

While body and mind can seem to be two distinct and separate things, from the Buddhist perspective of oneness, they are not. They are integral components of life as a whole that arise from the same essential source: the Mystic Law, or Nam-myoho-renge-kyo.

When we chant Nam-myoho-renge-kyo, we awaken the Buddha nature that exists within us and in everything around us. So, rather than thinking of the mind as comprising only desires, feelings, or conscience, and the body as a biomechanical form, we come to understand the interconnectedness of all life and phenomena, which have both material and spiritual aspects.

This is reflected in the word *nam* of Nam-myoho-renge-kyo, which indicates dedicating our life to the Mystic Law.

Nichiren Daishonin explains:

> "Dedication" refers to the element of physical form as it pertains to us, while "life" refers to the element of mind as it pertains to us. But the ultimate teaching tells us that form and mind are not two. (OTT, 3).

By chanting and practicing Buddhism for self and others, we activate our Buddha nature and elevate our life condition, bringing forth our inherent ability to harmonize the workings of our mind and body at the most essential level.

THE KEY TO A HEALTHY BODY AND MIND

Based on the oneness of body and mind, what's most important in forging a strong, healthy, and happy life is our resolve. President Ikeda explains:

> Life is inherently endowed with the marvellous capacity to convert even the negative into something positive. At the most basic level, one's life is created by one's own inner resolve, one's mind. This is even more true of a person with faith.[4]

Here, by "one's mind," President Ikeda means more than simply thoughts or ideas; he is stressing the importance having a powerful resolve that permeates one's heart, mind, and body.

When we experience illness or anxiety, which can easily take a mental or physical toll, it's helpful to know that we can chant and engage in our Buddhist practice to alleviate stress, develop resiliency, and strengthen our inner resolve.

In chanting, we tap the power of the Mystic Law within us and transform negative tendencies such as doubt, fear, anxiety, or anger into positive qualities like confidence, courage, wisdom, and appreciation. These help us take positive actions that propel us forward.

Founding Soka Gakkai president Tsunesaburo Makiguchi stated that by persevering in faith with a powerful determination to change "poison into medicine," we can gain great fortune and benefit, and become even healthier than before.[5] Here, "becoming healthier" can mean improving our physical and mental health, and it indicates our ability to create great value in any situation.

President Ikeda offers the following points for attaining a state of excellent health: "Chant daimoku, trusting in the power of the Gohonzon. Strive fearlessly and patiently. Refuse to accept defeat. Never retreat a single step. In the end, you are certain to triumph!"[6]

WHAT DOES THE ONENESS OF BODY AND MIND LOOK LIKE?

Anne O'Sullivan, an SGI member in Ireland, suffered from ulcerative colitis, an inflammatory bowel disease that caused crippling stomach pains and rapid weight loss, leading to surgeries and repeated hospital stays. She was later diagnosed with Crohn's disease, a chronic illness affecting her digestive tract.

Chanting, engaging in Buddhist activities, and studying Nichiren Daishonin's writings and President Ikeda's guidance, what she describes as her "constant companions," helped her rise above her frustration and hopelessness, and deepen her appreciation for life.

While she continues to deal with Crohn's disease, she says:

"From a certain perspective, I was 'unwell' before I became sick. My attitude toward myself was unhealthy, as I constantly looked outside myself for happiness, which always led to more feelings of dissatisfaction. It took my illness to make me realize that the source of true happiness is within myself. I now have complete conviction in the power of my prayers."[7]

Like O'Sullivan, countless SGI members are using their Buddhist practice to elevate their life condition and revolutionize their lives physically and spiritually, encouraging many others along the way.

CONCEPT EIGHTEEN

ONENESS OF GOOD AND EVIL
Transforming Evil Into the Highest Good

In thinking about Buddhism, many imagine a person of serenity, someone who spends time in a tranquil setting with a satisfied, knowing smile.

Nichiren Buddhist practice certainly helps us to maintain our composure and find peace and tranquility within. But rather than needing a tranquil setting, Buddhism teaches that to become such a person requires an ongoing and rigorous struggle, a willingness to challenge and overcome both internal and external evils.

The word *evil* may conjure various images and ideas. But Buddhism describes evil as that which essentially harms self and others[1] and is rooted in egoism, thinking only about one's personal interests.[2] It points to our fundamental ignorance, our innate delusion that causes us to doubt our potential for Buddhahood and to devalue ourselves and others.

In contrast, Buddhism describes good as that which benefits self and others. It is based on our fundamental nature of enlightenment, the genuine desire to lead all people to absolute happiness, or enlightenment.

The principle of the oneness of good and evil in Buddhism teaches that all phenomena possesses the potential for good and evil. While good and evil on their own have no substance, the oneness of good and evil is expressed only when evil functions to reveal good. If evil is simply allowed to persist in exerting its influence, it remains evil.

GOOD COMES FROM VANQUISHING EVIL

People are neither intrinsically good nor evil. Whether good or evil emerges from our lives depends on our life condition and intent. Anger, for instance, can function as good when directed toward evil actions such as oppression, cruelty, or violence. But if we lash out unfairly at others due to a bruised ego or pride, such anger functions as evil.

President Ikeda explains the importance of basing ourselves on faith (devotion to the happiness of self and others) rather than ambition (devotion to self). He states:

> A person of faith seeks self-mastery; a person of ambition or power seeks to control others. A person of faith takes action, works hard, and struggles to overcome his or her inner weakness; a person driven by a desire for power forces others to work for his own selfish purpose, never reflecting upon himself.[3]

Nichiren Daishonin writes, "One who is thoroughly awakened to the nature of good and evil from their roots to their branches and leaves is called a Buddha" (WND-1, 1121).

No matter our state of life, the evil of fundamental ignorance will constantly challenge us, internally and externally. When we know this, we can be ready to take on any situation, determined to transform everything into the greatest good.

President Ikeda says:

> If we perceive our inner evil but neglect efforts to conquer it, then our lives are instantaneously stained with evil. In that

sense, a good person is someone who struggles against evil. It is by fighting the evil around us that we eradicate evil within our lives and so purify them. That is the path of human revolution.[4]

Nichiren teaches that "the single word 'belief' is the sharp sword" that we can use to cut through fundamental ignorance (OTT, 119–20). Recognizing fundamental ignorance and challenging it with faith—chanting Nam-myoho-renge-kyo with determination and refusing to let difficulties defeat us—is the key to elevating our life state and transforming everything into the greatest good.

REFUSING TO BE DEFEATED

Examples of transforming evil into great good can be found throughout Buddhism's history.

Devadatta, Shakyamuni's cousin and disciple, fell victim to jealousy and ambition. He allied himself with a king in a plot to do away with the Buddha and create disunity in the Buddhist order. The True Word priest Ryokan repeatedly colluded with leaders in the Kamakura shogunate to persecute Nichiren and his disciples.

But both Shakyamuni and Nichiren transformed tumult into fuel for showing their true strength, revealing their Buddhahood and further spreading the correct practice of Buddhism.

President Ikeda says:

> The Buddha's state of life is such that no power or scheme can harm him. Devadatta's failed attempts to do away with Shakyamuni eloquently attest to this. We see the same in the case of Nichiren Daishonin. Even with the immense power of the ruling Kamakura shogunate at their disposal, the Daishonin's enemies could not make good on their schemes.[5]

More recently, the Soka Gakkai faced similar challenges in dealing with the Nichiren Shoshu priesthood. The priesthood distorted

Nichiren's teachings for their own self-serving interests and persecuted President Ikeda and Soka Gakkai members.

Similar to Shakyamuni and Nichiren, the Soka Gakkai transformed this intense challenge into a catalyst to clarify correct Buddhist practice in modern times.

In each era, genuine practitioners of the Mystic Law have faced evil while uniting and working for the highest good—to help all people reveal their Buddhahood. Continuing this noble effort, we are enacting the dynamic principle of the oneness of good and evil, in which even evil, when thoroughly confronted and overcome, can serve to strengthen and solidify the path to peace, tranquility, and happiness for all humanity.

CONCEPT NINETEEN

ONENESS OF LIFE AND ITS ENVIRONMENT
Winning Over Ourselves Brings Victory in All Other Realms

What did the hot dog vendor say when the Buddhist asked for change? "Change comes from within."

We may chuckle (or groan) at yet another Buddhist joke. But it assumes we are at least aware of an essential Nichiren Buddhist teaching: that changing our surroundings starts by changing our inner state of life.

It's easy to view oneself and one's environment as separate. Yet the Buddhist principle of the oneness of life and its environment offers a more profound view. This is expressed in Japanese as *esho-funi*.[1] *Esho* is a combination of *eho*, our environment, and *shoho*, meaning "living beings." *Funi*, which translates to "not two," indicates the oneness or profound interdependence of life and its environment.

Together, these components indicate that self and environment appear to be two distinct things but are inextricable on a deeper level (oneness).

In addition, *ho*, the second component of both *shoho* and *eho*, means "reward" or "effect." That is, the effects of good and bad causes we have accumulated from the past express themselves in all aspects of our present lives, as well as in our environment.

So our inner state of life affects the way we as individuals experience the world, our relationships, and our circumstances. Hence, changing any problem or situation starts with changing ourselves.

BUILDING A STRONG SELF IS KEY

The concept of the three realms of existence—a prime component of the principle three thousand realms in a single moment of life—serves as a basis for the oneness of life and its environment. The three realms help us understand life from three perspectives: (1) the realm of the five components (the individual); (2) the realm of living beings (society); and (3) the realm of the environment (the environment in which we live).

Of course, each person has different personality traits, family situations, and financial circumstances, and each lives under different societal and environmental conditions. Because all three realms of existence are intertwined, however, a problem in any one of these realms affects the others.

Most vital among the three is the internal realm of the individual. A transformation in our inner state of life affects the social and environmental realms.

Nichiren Daishonin states:

> If the minds of living beings are impure, their land is also impure, but if their minds are pure, so is their land. There are not two lands, pure or impure in themselves. The difference lies solely in the good or evil of our minds. (WND-1, 4)

"The good or evil of our minds" determines everything.

Buddhism describes "good" as that which upholds the dignity and equality of life—fundamental enlightenment—while "evil" is that which denigrates, devalues, and harms life—fundamental ignorance.

When motivated by things like greed, anger, and foolishness, we may take negative, destructive actions. Fortunately, our Buddhist practice helps us consistently work on bringing forth and strengthening the good within us.

When we chant Nam-myoho-renge-kyo, we tap our fundamental enlightenment and develop the clarity and resolve to break through any ignorance, delusion, or negativity that hinders our ability to treat ourselves and others with the utmost respect and compassion. President Ikeda says:

> We employ the strategy of the Lotus Sutra to triumph over inconceivably arduous circumstances and build strong selves that cannot be shaken by anything. As we win and win again, we are at the same time creating an environment of the most resplendent success and glory. In all things, life and environment are one. Therefore, by achieving self-mastery, we also achieve victory in our environment.[2]

THE ONENESS OF LIFE AND ENVIRONMENT IN ACTION

Earlier this year, the *World Tribune* interviewed SGI-USA member Asha Charles of Diego Martin, Trinidad and Tobago.[3]

After an economic downturn in 2007, robberies, gun violence, and other crimes escalated in Asha's neighborhood. Even the police disappeared from the streets.

Haunted each day by the thought of friends and neighbors getting attacked or shot, Asha, her mother, and local members sprang into action.

"We realized that any change in our community had to begin with a change in ourselves," she said. "We united around this determination to take back the neighborhood." They united in chanting many hours and studying Buddhism each day and sharing Buddhism with every young person they met.

It took a couple of years of such persistent efforts, but the police returned, the troublemakers moved out, and their community became safer and closer than ever.

Asha comments on their victory: "I've learned that living beings and the environment are a single integrated dynamic. And that when one person stands up with a vow to transform the environment, change is guaranteed. . . . Nothing is impossible with Nam-myoho-renge-kyo."

Asha and the members in Trinidad and Tobago wonderfully exemplify that a change in our resolve is the key to transforming our own lives, families, communities, and the world.

CONCEPT TWENTY

ONENESS OF MENTOR AND DISCIPLE
A Shared Commitment to Elevate Humanity

What is the purpose of Nichiren Buddhism? To awaken each person to their fullest potential and help each establish rich, fulfilling, genuinely happy lives. At the same time, its broader goal is to elevate the human condition, to create a harmonious and peaceful society that respects the sanctity of each person's life.

While individual happiness may seem "doable," some may see creating peace in today's chaotic and divisive world as too idealistic. Even if possible, such a grand and noble goal might not be achievable for generations.

To accomplish something of enduring value for humankind requires hope, determination, and passionate efforts maintained over successive generations far into the future. That is not and will never be easy. But having someone who has dedicated their life to doing so, who can stand as a model of such commitment and action, is extremely helpful.

This is why Buddhism stresses the importance of the mentor-disciple relationship.

All great revolutions have begun with the vision and resolve of one or a few people (mentors). Their efforts may have been hindered by harassment, imprisonment, or even death. Yet in revolutions that succeeded, there have always been disciples who inherited and worked hard to realize their mentor's vision.

President Ikeda explains:

> Without the mentor-disciple relationship, anything we undertake just ends with our own lifetime. . . . In contrast, the mentor-disciple relationship enables us to live a life connected to the great flow of humanity, a life like a mighty river, a life that is part of an unending relay race.
>
> Buddhism teaches the oneness of mentor and disciple. This is not a hierarchy, with the mentor above and the disciple below. Mentor and disciple share the same goal and advance together toward it. . . .
>
> Mentors and disciples are like runners in a relay race. They are pressing ahead, passing the baton forward on the shared path of justice, happiness, and peace for all humanity. The mentors run ahead to later pass the baton to the disciples.[1]

MENTOR AND DISCIPLE: THE WAY OF THE BUDDHA

A Buddha is a person awakened to the truth that all people are equally endowed with the Buddha nature or enlightened nature. Awakened to this truth, to the Mystic Law, the Buddha then strives to make all people aware of it.

A Buddha is not a superhuman or godlike figure but a human being, just like us. Therefore, the relationship between the Buddha and ordinary people is likened to that between a teacher and student, or mentor and disciple.

Unfortunately, in the centuries after Shakyamuni Buddha, this awareness gradually faded and the Buddha became a deified figure. But the Lotus Sutra corrects this mistaken view. The sutra's second chapter, "Expedient Means," expresses the Buddha's resolve "to make all persons equal to me, without any distinction between us" (LSOC, 70). The Buddha, as the mentor, strove to awaken all people, the disciples, to their own Buddhahood.

This simple yet profound teaching of universal enlightenment for all people in the Lotus Sutra was also recognized, taught, and spread by Nichiren Daishonin in the thirteenth century.

And, as the sutra predicted, as Nichiren and his disciples strove to spread this teaching of absolute equality, they faced intense persecution from government and religious authorities determined to keep ordinary people powerless and subservient.

The Lotus Sutra teaches the importance of respecting all human beings and winning over the devilish nature to look down on others.

Based on this spirit, the shared faith and struggle of mentor and disciple is found in striving together to spread the Mystic Law widely. While mentor and disciples are different, unique individuals, they are one and inseparable in the spirit and desire to awaken all people to their true power.

SEEKING A CORRECT MENTOR ENABLES US TO OVERCOME ALL CHALLENGES

In Buddhism, it is the disciple who chooses the mentor and takes action in line with the mentor's example and guidance. It's important, then, to choose a mentor who correctly practices Buddhism, selflessly dedicates their life to spreading the Law, and battles and wins over the negative functions that seek to hinder our efforts to awaken all people to their Buddhahood.

President Ikeda says, "Correct teachers of the Law can be identified by whether they have encountered hardships and opposition just like those described in the Lotus Sutra."[2]

It is through seeking our mentor as an example and making efforts to practice Buddhism for the happiness of self and others that we become people who take action to benefit others, thus achieving a magnificent inner transformation.

President Ikeda has said:

One person standing up to champion truth—as long as there is one such individual, people will not become confused. Everyone will experience great peace of mind. They will gather in support of that just cause, encouraging one another and advancing together. There is nothing more joyous than this eternal journey of kosen-rufu. There is nothing more exhilarating.[3]

NOTES

Concept 1
1. Daisaku Ikeda, *The Wisdom for Creating Happiness and Peace*, Part 1, *Happiness*, rev. ed. (Santa Monica, CA: World Tribune Press, 2021), 101.
2. Myoho-renge-kyo is written with five Chinese characters, while Nam-myoho-renge-kyo is written with seven (*nam* comprising two characters). Nichiren Daishonin often uses Myoho-renge-kyo synonymously with Nam-myoho-renge-kyo in his writings.
3. Daisaku Ikeda et al., *The Wisdom of the Lotus Sutra*, vol. 3 (Santa Monica, CA: World Tribune Press, 2011), 221.

Concept 2
1. Alexandre Dumas, *The Count of Monte Cristo* (London: Penguin Books, 2003), 160.
2. Nagarjuna: A Mahayana scholar thought to have lived between the years 150 and 250. His many writings elevated Mahayana Buddhism and had a major impact on Buddhism in China and Japan.
3. Daisaku Ikeda, *Toward a Century of Health* (Santa Monica, CA: World Tribune Press, 2022), 25.

Concept 3
1. Daisaku Ikeda, *Unlocking the Mysteries of Birth and Death* (Santa Monica, CA: Middleway Press, 2003), 162.
2. Ikeda, *Unlocking the Mysteries*, 164.
3. Ikeda, *Unlocking the Mysteries*, 160.

Concept 4
1. Daisaku Ikeda, *The Wisdom for Creating Happiness and Peace*, Part 2, *Human Revolution*, rev. ed. (Santa Monica, CA: World Tribune Press, 2022), 13.
2. Daisaku Ikeda, *The Wisdom for Creating Happiness and Peace*, Part 3, *Kosen-rufu and World Peace* (Santa Monica, CA: World Tribune Press, 2020), 42.

Concept 5
1. Vincent Harding and Daisaku Ikeda, *America Will Be!* (Cambridge, MA: Dialogue Path Press, 2013), 190.
2. Daisaku Ikeda et al., *The Wisdom of the Lotus Sutra*, vol. 3 (Santa Monica, CA: World Tribune Press, 2011), 252.
3. Daisaku Ikeda, *The New Human Revolution*, vol. 30 (Santa Monica, CA: World Tribune Press, 2021), 838–39.

Concept 6
1. *Living Buddhism*, February 2021, 60.
2. Daisaku Ikeda, *The New Human Revolution*, vol. 4, rev. ed. (Santa Monica, CA: World Tribune Press, 2019), 257.
3. Daisaku Ikeda, *Champions of Hope* (Santa Monica, CA: World Tribune Press, 2020, 42.
4. Daisaku Ikeda, *The New Human Revolution*, vol. 5, rev. ed. (Santa Monica, CA: World Tribune Press, 2019), 109.

Concept 7
1. Daisaku Ikeda, *The New Human Revolution*, vol. 25 (Santa Monica, CA: World Tribune Press, 2014), 163.
2. Ceremony in the Air: One of the three assemblies described in the Lotus Sutra. It spans chapters eleven through twenty-two of the sutra. The heart of this ceremony is the revelation of the Buddha's original enlightenment in the remote past and the transfer of the essence of the sutra to the Bodhisattvas of the Earth.
3. Daisaku Ikeda, *My Dear Friends in America*, 3rd. ed. (Santa Monica, CA: World Tribune Press, 2012), 99.

4. Ikeda, *My Dear Friends*, 99–100.
5. Daisaku Ikeda, *The World of Nichiren's Writings*, vol. 1 (Santa Monica, CA: World Tribune Press, 2022), 253.

Concept 8
1. Daisaku Ikeda, *Discussions on Youth*, new ed. (Santa Monica, CA: World Tribune Press, 2010), 299.
2. Daisaku Ikeda, *The Wisdom for Creating Happiness and Peace, Part 1, Happiness*, rev. ed. (Santa Monica, CA: World Tribune Press, 2021), 125.

Concept 9
1. Daisaku Ikeda et al., *The Wisdom of the Lotus Sutra*, vol. 3 (Santa Monica, CA: World Tribune Press, 2011), 17.
2. Ikeda, *Wisdom of the Lotus Sutra*, vol. 3, 17.
3. Ikeda, *Wisdom of the Lotus Sutra*, vol. 3, 18.

Concept 10
1. Saemon-no-jo refers to Shijo Kingo, a leading disciple of Nichiren Daishonin who accompanied him to Tatsunokuchi and resolved to die by his side. His full name and title were Shijo Nakatsukasa Saburo Saemon-no-jo Yorimoto. Kingo is an equivalent of the title Saemon-no-jo.
2. See Daisaku Ikeda et al., *The Wisdom of the Lotus Sutra*, vol. 4 (Santa Monica, CA: World Tribune Press, 2013), 50.
3. Daisaku Ikeda, "The Great Vow for the Happiness of All Humanity," *Living Buddhism*, January 2014, 8.
4. Daisaku Ikeda, "Ushering In a New Day of Hope," *World Tribune*, February 19, 2021, 3.

Concept 11
1. Six sense organs refer to the eyes, ears, nose, tongue, body, and mind.
2. Daisaku Ikeda, "The World of Nichiren's Writings," *Living Buddhism*, August 2003, 47.
3. Daisaku Ikeda, *The Wisdom for Creating Happiness and Peace*, Part 2, *Human Revolution*, rev. ed. (Santa Monica, CA: World Tribune Press, 2022), 40–41.

Concept 12

1. Ten Worlds: The Ten Worlds represent ten states of life. They are the worlds of (1) hell, (2) hungry spirits, (3) animals, (4) *asuras*, (5) human beings, (6) heavenly beings, (7) voice-hearers, (8) cause-awakened ones, (9) bodhisattvas, and (10) Buddhas.
2. Daisaku Ikeda, *The Wisdom for Creating Happiness and Peace*, Part 1, *Happiness*, rev. ed. (Santa Monica, CA: World Tribune Press, 2021), 48.

Concept 13

1. Daisaku Ikeda, *Discussions on Youth*, new ed. (Santa Monica, CA: World Tribune Press, 2010), 411.
2. The Great Teacher T'ien-t'ai (538–97), also known as Chih-i, was the founder of the T'ien-t'ai school in China and spread the Lotus Sutra in China. His lectures were compiled in such works as *The Profound Meaning of the Lotus Sutra*, *The Words and Phrases of the Lotus Sutra*, and *Great Concentration and Insight*.
3. For a detailed explanation of the ten factors of life, see Daisaku Ikeda, *The Heart of the Lotus Sutra* (Santa Monica, CA: World Tribune Press, 2013), 103–24.
4. The realm of the five components: an analysis of the nature of a living entity in terms of how it responds to its surroundings. The five components are (1) form, corresponding to the physical aspect of life, and the other four, which correspond to the spiritual aspect: (2) perception, (3) conception, (4) volition, and (5) consciousness.
5. Daisaku Ikeda, *The Wisdom for Creating Happiness and Peace*, Part 1, *Happiness*, rev. ed. (Santa Monica, CA: World Tribune Press, 2021), 78–79.

Concept 14

1. Daisaku Ikeda, *The Hope-Filled Teachings of Nichiren Daishonin* (Santa Monica, CA: World Tribune Press, 2009), 206.
2. Ikeda, *Hope-Filled Teachings*, 206.
3. Ikeda, *Hope-Filled Teachings*, 212.

Concept 15
1. Daisaku Ikeda, "The Buddhism of the Sun Illuminating the World," *Living Buddhism*, October 2021, 60.

Concept 16
1. Philip J. Ivanhoe et al., eds., *The Oneness Hypothesis* (New York: Columbia University Press, 2018), inside cover text.
2. The Great Teacher Miao-lo (711–82), also known as the Great Teacher Ching-his, after his birthplace. A patriarch of the T'ien-t'ai school in China. He is revered as the school's restorer. His commentaries on T'ien-t'ai's three major works are titled *The Annotations on "The Profound Meaning of the Lotus Sutra," The Annotations on "The Words and Phrases of the Lotus Sutra,"* and *The Annotations on "Great Concentration and Insight."*
3. For a brief discussion of the ten onenesses, go to: https://www.nichirenlibrary.org/en/dic/Content/T/63.
4. Daisaku Ikeda, *The Flower of Chinese Buddhism* (Santa Monica, CA: Middleway Press, 2009), 146.
5. Daisaku Ikeda, "Soka: A Realm Overflowing With Hope and Joy," *World Tribune*, January 22, 2010, special insert, F.

Concept 17
1. "Brain Basics: Know Your Brain," https://www.ninds.nih.gov/Disorders/Patient-Caregiver-Education/Know-Your-Brain, accessed on March 1, 2022.
2. "The Gut-Brain Connection," https://www.health.harvard.edu/diseases-and-conditions/thegut-brain-connection, accessed on March 1, 2022.
3. "Using Music to Tune the Heart," https://www.health.harvard.edu/newsletter_article/using-music-to-tune-the-heart, accessed on March 1, 2022.
4. Daisaku Ikeda, *Humanism and the Art of Medicine* (Kuala Lumpur, Malaysia: Soka Gakkai Malaysia, 1999), 56.
5. Daisaku Ikeda, *The Five Eternal Guidelines of the Soka Gakkai* (Santa Monica, CA: World Tribune Press, 2017), 55–56.
6. Daisaku Ikeda, *The Wisdom for Creating Happiness and Peace, Part 1, Happiness*, rev. ed. (Santa Monica, CA: World Tribune Press, 2021), 252.

7. Anne O'Sullivan, "My Tailor-Made Disease," *https://www.sokaglobal.org/practicing-buddhism/personal-experiences/my-tailor-made-disease*, accessed on March 1, 2022.

Concept 18

1. See "oneness of good and evil," The Soka Gakkai Dictionary of Buddhism, *https://www.nichirenlibrary.org/en/dic/Content/O/23*.
2. See Daisaku Ikeda et al., *The Wisdom of the Lotus Sutra*, vol. 3 (Santa Monica, CA: World Tribune Press, 2013), 80.
3. Ikeda, *Wisdom of the Lotus Sutra*, vol. 3, 72.
4. Ikeda, *Wisdom of the Lotus Sutra*, vol. 3, 76.
5. Ikeda, *Wisdom of the Lotus Sutra*, vol. 3, 73–74.

Concept 19

1. See "oneness of life and its environment" in *The Soka Gakkai Dictionary of Buddhism*, *https://www.nichirenlibrary.org/en/dic/Content/O/24*, accessed on March 1, 2022.
2. Daisaku Ikeda, "Men: Champions of Kosen-rufu," *World Tribune*, March 13, 2009, special insert, D.
3. See "Taking Back Our Neighborhood With Powerful Daimoku," *World Tribune*, June 4, 2021, 10.

Concept 20

1. Daisaku Ikeda, *The Wisdom for Creating Happiness and Peace*, Part 3, *Kosen-rufu and World Peace* (Santa Monica, CA: World Tribune Press, 2020), 176.
2. Daisaku Ikeda, *The Wisdom for Creating Happiness and Peace*, Part 3, 192.
3. Daisaku Ikeda, "The World of Nichiren's Writings," *Living Buddhism*, October 2003, 39.